"One of the greatest living teachers of Dzogchen, His Holiness the Dalai Lama, explains one of the most profound texts of this tradition (Patrul Rinpoche's *Three Keys*), and the teaching is translated by one of America's leading scholars, Jeffrey Hopkins. Does it get any better than this?"

> —JOSÉ I. CABEZÓN,
> author of *The Buddha's Doctrine and the Nine Vehicles*

"Despite the alleged sectarianism of Tibetan Buddhism, there has been a long history of mutual influence and inspiration across the traditions. Over the course of the past four hundred years, one of the most famous has been the study and practice of Dzogchen by the lineage of the Dalai Lamas. It continues to the present day, as this volume eloquently attests."

> —DONALD S. LOPEZ JR.,
> author of *From Stone to Flesh: A Short History of the Buddha*

The

HEART

of

MEDITATION

Discovering Innermost Awareness

THE DALAI LAMA

Translated and edited by Jeffrey Hopkins
from oral teachings

A teaching on Patrul Rinpoche's
Three Keys Penetrating the Core

SHAMBHALA
BOULDER
2016

Shambhala Publications, Inc.
4720 Walnut Street
Boulder, Colorado 80301
www.shambhala.com

9 8 7 6 5 4 3 2 1

FIRST EDITION
Printed in the United States of America

♾ This edition is printed on acid-free paper that meets the
American National Standards Institute z39.48 Standard.
♻ This book is printed on 30% postconsumer recycled paper.
For more information please visit www.shambhala.com.

Distributed in the United States by Penguin Random House LLC
and in Canada by Random House of Canada Ltd

Designed by Steve Dyer

LIBRARY OF CONGRESS CATALOGING-IN-PUBLICATION DATA

Names: Bstan-'dzin-rgya-mtsho, Dalai Lama XIV,
1935– author. | Hopkins, Jeffrey.
Title: The heart of meditation: discovering innermost awareness /
The Dalai Lama; translated and edited by Jeffrey Hopkins.
Description: First edition. | Boulder: Shambhala, 2016. |
Includes bibliographical references and index.
Identifiers: LCCN 2015021940 | ISBN 9781559394536 (hardback)
Subjects: LCSH: Rdzogs-chen. |
BISAC: RELIGION / Buddhism / Tibetan. |
RELIGION / Buddhism / Rituals & Practice. |
RELIGION / Buddhism / Sacred Writings.
Classification: LCC BQ 7935.B774 H45 2016 | DDC 294.3/4435—dc23
LC record available at http://lccn.loc.gov/2015021940

CONTENTS

CONTENTS

PART FOUR *The Old and New*
Translation Schools Compared

CONTENTS

FOREWORD

This is an extraordinary book in which His Holiness the Dalai Lama provides intimate details on meditation. In preparation for a teaching in London in the summer of 1984 on a visionary poem by a profound Tibetan yogi, His Holiness taught me this text in his Private Office in Dharamsala, India, since I was to serve as his interpreter for the public talk. In this book, I have interwoven these private teachings with the Dalai Lama's seminar lectures in Camden Centre, which affords readers a compelling picture about how to put themselves into a deep state beyond the confining coverings of too much thought, released into the naked core of innermost mind. The aim is to make use of the space between thoughts to experience a deeper level of basic awareness and bring it to the fore, realizing the floor of all conscious experience.

The book is structured in four parts. In the first, the Dalai Lama provides the context of the extraordinarily direct instructions of the poem by fleshing out the advice given at its end to train in empathy for all beings and in knowledge of the nature of all phenomena — persons and objects. In the second, he introduces the system of the Great Completeness and identifies innermost awareness as the fundamental principle common to all orders of Tibetan Buddhism. In the third, he comments on the inspired poem, opening up its meaning by expanding on the three keys that are its essential message — how to identify innermost awareness within yourself, how to maintain contact with innermost awareness in all states, and how to release yourself from too much thought. You will easily see the common thread of the first three parts: by expanding compassionate empathy for all beings, you break down barriers that draw us into myriad counterproductive destructive thoughts and actions, and by exploring the nature of the mind, oneself, and objects, you undermine the lure of their seductive concreteness, making it possible to make use of the space between thoughts and allow a deeper mind to manifest. In the fourth, he provides more explanation about special spiritual topics such as the two truths — conventional and ultimate, purity from the start, inward and outward luminosity, the gradual diminishment of conceptuality and the increase of actualization of innermost awareness, and identifying the clear light in the midst of any consciousness. The four parts reinforce each other; therefore you may want to read around in them at will.

Let me add that the stay in London for the lectures in Camden Centre was most interesting for me. My ancestors on both sides, the Hopkins and Adams, were in America from the time of the Revolution and both traced their roots to England, and my fascination with the ancestral home stemmed mainly from wanting to see if I felt any bond at all with the English. The Dalai Lama was staying at the home of the pacifist, ecumenist, and feminist the Very Reverend Edward F. Carpenter, dean of Westminster (from 1974 to 1986), and his wife Lilian, both of whom I quickly found to be very warm and open. I was put up at the Liberal Club a few blocks away, having to walk past Downing Street, home and office of the prime minister, where my inner juvenile delinquent would make me take a few steps toward Number 10 and pause long enough to make the security edgy.

On July 2, Lilian Carpenter guided me through the magisterial but awfully gray Westminster Abbey with pleasant and sometimes jovial conversation. We had a lovely time, enjoying each other's company, all the while identifying the history of the great leaders of England commemorated around us in great blocks of stone, though I have to admit that I felt more and more estranged from my ancestors, despite feeling more and more at home with her.

The next day I returned to Westminster Abbey to interpret for His Holiness. A boys choir sang with the

angelic voices of youth, and His Holiness was introduced. The first sentence he spoke to the assembled audience in this great abbey was in Tibetan: "I do not care
about buildings," and he waved his hand ever so slightly
to indicate that he meant this very building, sweeping
to heaven above us. This, in effect, was his first public
statement in London; he said no more, pausing for my
translation. I had no idea where he was going, what was
to follow, so I had no context. I am a firm believer in
translating exactly what a lama says, although context
allows for some choice of words. But here I had none;
my only context was how much this building meant to
the audience! But that did not matter. At issue was his
point, so I had to translate exactly what he said, and I
did. This was his second visit to England, but the first
was not for teaching, so the audience had no context
either. The response seemed to be totally flat; to look
at their faces, it was as if he had not said anything. His
Holiness continued, "My interest is in what is happening
in your mind, your heart." When he says this nowadays,
there is instant recognition, a deep sense of acknowl-
edgment, but then and there in Westminster Abbey, as
I watched the audience, their response still seemed to be
flat. If anything was happening, it was underneath, but
in time it was obvious that the audience warmed.

His Holiness was speaking his mind, and slowly the
world has seen and appreciated this marvel, this person

who calls us to look within. The message has stayed the same, unfolding in detail as he has become the Lama of the World.

May I tell you a funny story? Prior to arriving in London, as the Dalai Lama and his party traveled to Edinburgh, Glasgow, Coventry, and so on, we kept hearing, "He is going to speak in Royal Albert Hall on July 5!" I got the impression that this is the "Wow! Hall" of Great Britain. And, indeed, with its five curving balconies that embrace the stage, so that no seat is far away, thus affording a strong sense of intimacy, it is magnificent! The stage curves out into the audience, and they can almost put their elbows on it. With His Holiness and myself in the middle, to our left, at a distance, was a fellow in the first row who, about two-thirds into the talk, opened a can of pop with a whole lot of a fizz. As usual, His Holiness was not at all fazed, but since I always figured I was a first line of defense, standing so close to him, I wondered if the fellow intended to give him a soda bath. But nothing happened, and the talk went along fine. The dean said his goodbyes, and as we were walking back behind the stage, I whispered to a couple of Tibetan security personnel to be careful about the fellow in the first row with a soda. The security heard "with a sword," and they went into extra special precaution mode! I was later upbraided and then teased for unclear whispering.

Following the talk at Royal Albert Hall on "Peace of Mind, Peace in Action," which was very warmly received, His Holiness returned to the much smaller venue at Camden Centre in London, where the day before he had begun a four-day seminar series on the central Buddhist doctrine of interdependence. At the end of that series, he delivered a series of five lectures on the inspired poem that is at the heart of the present book.

The book is very rich and reflects the depth of Tibetan meditative and reflective culture, infused with kindness and practicality. It is a shining example of how this great Tibetan civilization that has had such enormous influence throughout much of Asia continues to benefit the world.

JEFFREY HOPKINS, PhD
President, UMA Institute of Tibetan Studies
Emeritus Professor of Tibetan Studies,
University of Virginia

PART ONE

The Buddhist Path

My Focus

MUCH OF THE world is now connected by a web of electronic communication and instant information. In the twenty-first century, our global economy has made nations and their people even more dependent upon one another. In ancient times, trade between nations was not necessary. Today, it is impossible to remain isolated, so if nations do not have mutual respect, problems are bound to arise. Although there are grave signs of trouble between poorer and richer nations, and between poorer and richer groups within nations, these economic rifts can be healed by a stronger sense of global interdependence and responsibility. The people of one nation must consider the people of other nations and those within their own nation to be like brothers and sisters who deserve the right to progress freely.

Despite the best efforts of world leaders, crises keep erupting. Wars kill innocent people; the elderly and children die continuously. Many soldiers who are fighting are not there by their own initiative; real suffering is experienced by these innocent soldiers, which is very sad. The sale of weapons — thousands and thousands of types of arms and ammunition — by manufacturers in big countries fuels the violence, but more dangerous than guns or bombs are hatred, lack of compassion, and lack of respect for the rights of others. As long as hatred dwells in the human mind, real peace is impossible.

We must do everything we can to stop war and to rid the world of nuclear weapons. When I visited Hiroshima, where the first atomic bomb was dropped, and saw the actual spot and heard the stories of survivors, my heart was deeply moved. How many people died in a single moment! How many more were injured! How much pain and desolation nuclear war creates! Yet look at how much money is still spent on weapons of mass destruction! It is shocking, an immeasurable disgrace.

Advancements in science and technology have indeed greatly benefited humankind, but not without a price. While, for example, we enjoy the development of jet airplanes that make it possible to easily travel the world, enormously destructive weapons have also been created. No matter how beautiful or remote their homelands, many people live in constant fear of a very real threat: thousands upon thousands of nuclear warheads aimed at them, poised for attack, or even a single nuclear weapon smuggled into a city. However, human beings must let them loose, and thus human intention is ultimately responsible.

The only way to achieve lasting peace is through mutual trust, respect, love, and kindness. The only way. Attempts by global powers to dominate one another through competition in armaments — whether nuclear, chemical, biological, or conventional — are counterproductive. How can a world full of hatred and anger achieve real peace?

External peace is impossible without inner peace. It is noble to work at external solutions, but they cannot be successfully implemented so long as people have hatred and anger in their minds. This is where profound change has to begin. Individually, we have to work to transform the basic perspectives on which our feelings depend. We can do so only through training, by engaging in practice with the aim of gradually reorienting the way we perceive ourselves and others.

The desperate state of our world calls us to action. Each of us has a responsibility to try to help at the deeper level of our common humanity. Unfortunately, humanity is too often sacrificed in defense of ideology. This is absolutely wrong. Political systems actually should benefit human beings, but, just as money does, they can control us instead of work for us.

If, with a warm heart and patience, we can consider the views of others and exchange ideas in calm discussion, we will find points of agreement. It is our responsibility — out of love and compassion for humankind — to seek harmony among nations, ideologies, cultures, ethnic groups, and economic and political systems.

When we truly recognize the oneness of all humankind, our motivation to find peace will grow stronger. In the deepest sense, we are really sisters and brothers, so we must share each other's suffering. Mutual respect, trust, and concern for one another's welfare is our best hope for lasting world peace.

Of course, national leaders have a special responsibility in this area, but every individual must also take the initiative, regardless of religious belief. Just by being human, by seeking to gain happiness and to avoid suffering, we are citizens of this planet. We all are responsible for creating a better future.

To achieve a friendly attitude, a warm heart, respect for the rights of others, and concern for their welfare, we must train the mind. The essential objective of mental training is to cultivate an attitude of compassion and calm — a state of mind particularly crucial in human society today because of its power to yield true harmony among nations, races, and people from diverse religious, political, and economic systems. With a compassionate and calm mind, we can develop the will, the drive, to bring about change.

Do you agree? Do you think this is nonsense? I am just a Buddhist monk. What I am saying comes from my own practice, which is limited. But I try to implement these ideas in my daily life, especially when I face problems. Of course, I fail sometimes. Sometimes I get irritated. Occasionally, I use a harsh word, but when I do, immediately I feel, "Oh, this is wrong." I feel this because I have internalized the practices of compassion and wisdom.

When I was only fifteen, the Chinese Communists invaded eastern Tibet, and within a year, the Tibetan government decided that I should direct Tibet's affairs of state. It was a difficult period as we watched our freedoms being eroded, and in 1959, I was forced to escape from the capital under cover of night. In exile in India, we faced problems daily, ranging from our need to adjust to the vastly different climate to our need to reestablish cultural institutions. My spiritual practice gave me an outlook that made it possible to keep searching for solutions without losing sight of the fact that we are all humans led astray by wrong ideas and united by common bonds, ready for improvement.

This has taught me that the perspectives of compassion, calm, and insight are essential to daily life and must be cultivated in daily practice. Trouble is bound to come, so cultivating the right attitude is crucial. Anger diminishes our power to distinguish right from wrong, and this ability is one of the highest human attributes. If it is lost, we are lost. Sometimes it is necessary to respond strongly, but this can be done without anger. Anger is not necessary. It has no value. Compassion and calm are what make long-lasting strong will viable.

I call compassion a global requirement. The mental peace of a consistent compassionate outlook is a basic need for all humankind. For students, politicians, engineers, scientists, homemakers, doctors, teachers, lawyers — for all people at every stage of life — a healthy, compassionate motivation is the foundation of healthy growth.

Most people nowadays who have had contact with Tibetans like them, saying that Tibetans have good character and that even though they are in a state of unusual suffering, having lost their country to an invasion, they remain relaxed. Some think that this is just the nature of the Tibetan people, but most understand that this arises from a mode of thinking, a willingness to use bad circumstances for spiritual growth. Because of this, they are not distressed, and their inner freedom from anxiety appears outwardly in the form of an easygoing manner. This is due to the teaching of compassion, which was widely disseminated in Tibet.

There is great advantage in practicing whatever degree of compassion we can. It is also very important to make wishes aspiring to be able to act more compassionately in the future. For any activity related to human society, compassion and love are vital, whether one is a politician, businessperson, social worker, scientist, engineer, and so on. If people carry out their work with good motivation, that work becomes an instrument for human benefit. On the other hand, if people utilize their profession not with this motive but out of selfishness or with anger, the profession becomes distorted. Instead of bringing benefit to humankind, the knowledge gained in the profession brings more disaster. So compassion is essential.

I know from my own experience that it is possible to change inner attitudes and improve the human mind. Though it is colorless, shapeless, and sometimes weak, the human mind can become stronger than steel. To train the mind, we must exercise the patience and determination it takes to shape that steel. If we practice improving our mind with a strong will and fortitude by trying, trying, trying, then no matter how many difficulties we may encounter at the beginning, we will succeed. With patience, and practice, and time, change will come. Do not be discouraged, but be courageous to enable implementation of whatever you can.

Empathy

The Basic Practice

In the next three chapters, I will say a little about the Buddhist spiritual path, which is the practice of empathy, meditation, and knowledge. The first, empathy — kindness or compassion — is the basis of Buddhism. Within having the same motivation of compassion, love, kindness, tolerance, and self-discipline, there are different philosophies and different methods among the various types of Buddhism, but the ultimate goal is to help all sentient beings. Buddhism is rich, with many explanations of techniques for developing, training in, and implementing compassion.

In the beginning of spiritual practice, the main essence is not to harm others. Nonviolence, or not harming others, is the root; thus compassion is the basic approach. Then, we expand our perspective to serve others, to help others, based on restraining selfishness. Compassion has become more mature. The practice of compassion at the beginning, when our capacities to help others are still not developed, is not to harm others, but then when those capacities have developed, it is to go to others to help them. Thus, in both these cases the basic teaching is compassion.

Essential to this is inner development, and so it is important to know how to generate it. There is an "I" that exists in dependence upon mind and body and that all of us conceive innately. This sense of "I" is a natural, innate, correct conception, and on the basis of it, we come to want happiness and not want suffering. These wishes too are correct and lead us to seek to gain happiness and avoid suffering. The attainment of happiness is a natural right, justified and validated simply by the fact that we naturally and correctly want happiness and do not want suffering.

Everyone has this same feeling of wanting happiness, and on that basis, everyone has equally the right to obtain happiness and remove suffering. Now, a question is to be posed. I am just a single person, whereas others are infinite in number. Our condition is the same in that we all want happiness. The only difference between us is in number — I am single whereas others are limitless. Thus the question is: Should everyone be used for my attainment of happiness, or should I work to gain happiness for others?

Therefore, the simplest method for generating compassion is this:

Visualize yourself in the middle as a neutral person. On your left side, visualize other beings, at least ten or fifteen or even a hundred; imagine needy people in poor condition. On your right side, visualize yourself again but as selfish, overly proud, and never thinking of others' welfare but only of your own welfare. In the middle, you remain as a third person evaluating. Both the single selfish person on the right and the group of destitute people on the left want happiness and do not want suffering; both have an equal right to be happy and to get rid of suffering. Which side would you, as the evaluator, choose?

This is one way to change our attitude toward others.

Another way is to reflect on the fact that the very nature of human society is that it is impossible for a person to exist in complete isolation. We are by nature interdependent, and since we must live together, why not do so with a positive attitude, a good mind? Why is it that instead of this we feel hatred for each other and bring more trouble to the world?

From the depths of our being, we need to view self-centeredness as faulty. Up until now, self-cherishing and its partner, ignorance, have dwelled in the center of our heart. Whether as a bug or as a higher being, self-cherishing has molded our outlook, with ignorance egging it on, so we have sought our own happiness as much as we could. But most of those actions intended to bring us happiness have only created a mess.

If we consider and reflect on ordinary events in the world situation today, we will see that the type of ruination that the world is undergoing is due to self-cherishing. The troubles that we are in, driven by self-cherishing, are not just limited to this lifetime, but are something in which we have been sunk since beginningless time. As the Indian scholar-yogi Shantideva says in his *Guide to the Bodhisattva's Way of Life*, we should consider just what kind of morass that self-cherishing has got us into, and compare this to the marvelous qualities and wonderful state of altruism that arises out of cherishing others. Compare these two, and you will easily see which is preferable.

From this viewpoint, this type of reflection is very useful to society these days, particularly when there is the danger of the human problems of unrest, violence, terrorism, and war, for under these circumstances, the force of compassion, the force of love and kindness, is essential. The harmony and friendship that we need in our families, schools, communities, nations, and world can be achieved only through compassion and kindness.

By helping one another, with concern and respect, we can solve many problems easily. Harmony cannot thrive in a climate of mistrust, cheating, bullying, and mean-spirited competition.

Success through intimidation and violence is temporary at best; its trifling gains only create new problems. This is why just a couple of decades after the enormous human tragedy of the First World War, the Second World War was fought, and millions more people were killed. After that, conflicts erupted on a continuous basis, one after another, until in this new millennium, the world is beset by a number of simultaneous, long-lasting bloodlettings. If we examine our lengthy history of hatred and anger, we see the obvious need to find a better way. We can solve our problems only through truly peaceful means — not just peaceful words but a peaceful mind and heart. In this way, we will have a better world.

Is this possible? Fighting, cheating, and bullying have trapped us in our present situation, heightened by technological innovation; now we need training in new practices to find a way out. It may seem impractical and idealistic, but we have no alternative to compassion, recognizing human value and the oneness of humanity: this is the only way to achieve lasting happiness. Compassion centers around being concerned with others, and it leads to a willingness to help according to our own ability.

I travel from country to country with this sense of oneness. I have trained my mind for decades, so when I meet people from different cultures, there are no barriers. I am convinced that despite different cultures and different political and economic systems, we are all basically the same. The more people I meet, the stronger my conviction becomes that the oneness of humanity, founded on understanding and respect, is a realistic and viable basis for our conduct.

Wherever I go, this is what I speak about. I believe that the practice of compassion and love — a genuine sense of sisterhood and brotherhood — is the universal religion. It does not matter whether you are a Buddhist or a Christian, Hindu, Muslim, or Jew, or whether you practice religion at all. What matters is the feeling of oneness with humankind.

· 3 ·

Meditation

Channeling the Force of Mind

To DEVELOP SPIRITUAL qualities such as love, compassion, and altruism to their fullest, meditation is needed. At present, our minds are too scattered, and once the mind is scattered, its force is limited. If we channel it, then, like water, it becomes forceful. Thus, one type of meditation is for developing a calm abiding of the mind, whereas the other type is for developing special insight in order to investigate the nature of reality. Let us begin with the first type.

If we do not have concentration in which the mind is unfluctuatingly stable and clear, the faculty of wisdom cannot know its object, just as it is, in all its subtleties. Therefore, it is necessary to have concentration. In the practice of concentration, the two main unfavorable factors preventing its development are laxity and excitement; as antidotes to these, we need to have mindfulness and introspection.

To describe briefly how these are achieved: When we meditate, first of all there is an object of observation that is either an external object or the mind itself. When the mind itself is taken as the object of observation, the practice is more profound.

In terms of posture, sit in either the full or half crosslegged posture. Use a cushion that is such that your rear is higher — the effect is that no matter how much meditation is cultivated you do not become tired. Your backbone is to be straightened like an arrow; your neck is to be bent just a little downward; aim your eyes over the nose to the front; touch your tongue to the roof of the mouth; leave your lips and teeth as usual, and leave your arms a little loose, not forcing them against the body. Put the hands in the position of meditative equipoise — the left hand below the right and the two thumbs touching, making a triangle the base of which is about four finger-widths below the navel.

If your mind is involved with desire or hatred, it is necessary to engage in a technique to loosen from this disturbance. Meditation on the inhalation and exhalation of the breath up to a count of twenty-one is the prime means for doing so. Since the mind cannot have two modes of apprehension simultaneously, this meditation causes the former disturbance to fade. Then, it is necessary to form a virtuous motivation — mainly compassion, altruism, wishing to help others.

To concentrate on the mind itself: Do not let your mind think on what has happened in the past or let it chase after things that might happen in the future; rather, leave the mind vivid, without any constructions, just as it is. When you remain this way, you understand that the mind, like a mirror, is such that any object, any conception, is capable of appearing under certain circumstances, like reflections, for the entity of the mind has a nature of mere luminosity and knowing, mere experience.

According to a basic Buddhist insight, the mind is essentially luminous and knowing. Therefore, emotional problems do not reside in the mind's essence; counterproductive attitudes are temporary, superficial, and can be removed. If distressing emotions such as anger were in the very nature of the mind, then from its inception, the mind would always have to be angry. Obviously, this is not so. Only under certain circumstances do we become angry, and when those circumstances are not present, anger is not present either.

What are the circumstances that serve as a basis for generating anger, or hatred? When we get angry, the object of our anger appears more awful than what is actually there. We get angry because the person has harmed, is harming, or will harm us or our friend.

What is this "I" that is being harmed?

We feel that both the subject, "I," and the object, the enemy, are solid and independent. Because we accept these appearances as inherently established, anger is generated. However, if at that first flash of rage, you make use of reason to examine

"Who am I? Who is this one who is being hurt? What is the enemy? Is the enemy the body? Is the enemy mind?"

this solidly existing enemy who previously seemed to be inherently created as something to get angry at and this I who was inherently created to be hurt seem to disappear. And the anger breaks apart.

Think about it. We get angry at what foils our desires. Anger is fomented by the misconception that the object and yourself are established this way, as enemy and victim, in and of themselves. Hatred is not part of the mind's foundation. It is an attitude without a valid foundation.

However, love is validly founded in truth. When, over a long period of time, an attitude that has a valid foundation competes with an attitude that does not, the one with the valid foundation will overwhelm the other. Therefore, qualities that depend on the mind can be increased limitlessly, and as you increase attitudes that counter distressing emotions, their unfavorable counterparts decrease, finally becoming extinguished altogether. Since the mind has an essential nature of luminosity and knowing, all of us have the fundamental equipment necessary to attain enlightenment.

Identifying the Mind

About twenty years ago when I was in Ladakh, India, performing a series of meditations, I had a statue of Shakyamuni Buddha before me, as is still my custom. The gold leaf at the heart of the statue had worn away, and thus that area was brownish in color. Looking at the heart of the statue, which had no attractive color, watching my mind, eventually thought stopped, and for a short period I felt the luminous and knowing nature of the mind. Subsequently recollecting this, the experience would return.

It is very helpful in daily practice to identify the nature of the mind and concentrate on it. However, it is hard to catch hold of the mind because it is hidden beneath our own scattered thoughts. As a technique to identify the basic nature of the mind, first stop remembering what happened in the past, then stop thinking about what might happen in the future — let the mind flow of its own accord without the overlay of thought.

Let the mind rest in its natural state and observe it for a while.

When, for instance, you hear a noise, between the time of hearing it and conceptualizing its source, you can sense a state of mind that is devoid of thought but not asleep, in which the object is a reflection of the mind's luminosity and knowing. At such a point, the basic nature of the mind can be grasped. In the beginning, when you are not used to this practice, it is quite difficult, but in time the mind appears like clear water. Try to stay with this state of mind without being distracted by conceptual thoughts, and become accustomed to it.

Practice this meditation in the early morning, when your mind has awakened and is clear, but your senses are not yet fully operating. It helps not to have eaten too much the night before, or to have slept too much — your sleep will be lighter, and this makes the mind lighter and sharper the next morning. If you eat too much, your sleep can be thick and heavy, almost like a corpse. In my own daily routine, I eat my fill at breakfast and lunch but just a little bit at night — less than half a cup of crackers — then I go to bed early and rise at three-thirty in the morning to begin meditation.

See if paying attention to the nature of the mind early in the morning makes your mind more alert throughout the day. Your thoughts certainly will be more tranquil.

If you are able to practice a little meditation every day, withdrawing from this scattered mind, your memory will improve. The conceptual mind that runs on thinking of good things, bad things, and so forth, will get a rest. A little nonconceptuality can provide a much-needed vacation.

Technique

1. Do not think about what happened in the past or what might happen in the future.
2. Let the mind flow of its own accord without thought.
3. Observe the mind's nature of luminous clarity.
4. Stay with this experience for a while.

You can even practice this while lying in bed in the morning, your mind awake but your senses not yet fully engaged.

When you identify the nature of the mind as mere luminosity and knowing, hold on to that experience — the mere luminosity and knowingness — and stay with it by way of mindfulness and introspection.

That is how to use the mind itself as an object of observation in the process of achieving concentrated meditation. If, rather than the mind, you use an external object of observation such as the body of Buddha, or the god of wisdom Manjushri, first take a good look at a well-designed image, and then visualize it mentally, causing an internal image of it to appear to the mind. Whether the object of observation is internal, the mind, or external, such as Buddha's body, once you mentally locate it, cause the mind to stay vividly on that object.

· 4 ·

Knowledge

The Purpose of Concentration

WHAT IS THE purpose in achieving such concentrated attention? It is not just for the sake of gaining a mind of higher levels of concentration by temporarily suppressing manifest coarse afflictive emotions. Rather, the purpose of meditative stabilization is to serve as a basis for achieving supramundane special insight realizing selflessness, the emptiness of inherent existence, through which afflictive emotions can be removed completely and forever.

The reason for cultivating the wisdom realizing the emptiness of inherent existence is that even if you have mere concentration, it cannot harm the misconception that objects exist in and of themselves. A union of concentration and wisdom is needed.

To generate the wisdom realizing selflessness in your

mental continuum, it is necessary to realize the meaning of emptiness. Whereas meditating on faith means that faith is cultivated in the sense of causing the mind to become faithful, to be generated into an entity of faith, meditating on selflessness means that selflessness, emptiness, is taken as an *object* of meditation, as the object of your mind. To do that, it is necessary to know what selflessness, emptiness, is.

As is clear in Nagarjuna's *Fundamental Treatise on the Middle*, phenomena are not said to be empty because of being nonexistent or unable to perform functions. Rather, all phenomena are empty because of being dependent; they are what we call in Buddhist philosophy dependent-arisings. Nagarjuna did not give as the reason why phenomena are empty that they are unable to be effective but, instead, that they are dependent-arisings. From this, it can be understood that the meaning of emptiness is the meaning of dependent-arising.

Since things are dependently established, there is nothing that is established independently. Dependent and independent are explicitly mutually exclusive, a dichotomy; thus, once things are dependently established, they are definitely not independent. Independence, non-dependence on others — that is, establishment under the object's own power — is called "self" in Buddhism; because it does not exist, we speak of selflessness.

According to the highest school of Buddhist philosophy, which embodies Nagarjuna's thought exactly as it is, there are two types of selflessness: selflessness of persons and selflessness of other phenomena. These are divided only by way of the substrata — persons and other phenomena — that are without self, independent existence, and not by way of a difference in the emptiness of these two. Both persons and other phenomena lack independent existence, which is to say, they lack existing in their own right, from their own side without depending on other factors such as causes and conditions or their own constituents.

To ascertain the meaning of selflessness, in general you must engage in analytical meditation, reflectively analyzing with reasoning. This is why Nagarjuna's *Fundamental Treatise on the Middle* presents many reasonings, all for the sake of proving from many viewpoints that all phenomena are empty of being established under their own power, empty of inherent existence, and utilizing these reasonings in meditation.

The *Questions of Kashyapa Chapter* in the *Pile of Jewels Sutra* says that forms are not empty because of emptiness, forms themselves are empty. Therefore, emptiness does not mean that a phenomenon is empty of being some other object but means that it itself is empty of its own inherent existence, a type of exaggerated existence that we add on top of how phenomena actually exist. Thus, objects are empty of this exaggerated status, this overblown reification that we lend to phenomena.

Begin with Yourself

Since it is the individual person who undergoes pleasure and pain, makes trouble, and accumulates karma — all the noise and the mess being made by the self — analysis should begin with yourself. Then, when you understand that you yourself are without this overblown status, you can extend this realization to the things that you enjoy, undergo, and make use of. In this sense, the person is the principal subject of analysis.

Can you remember a time when you did something awful and your mind thought, "I really made a mess of things"? At that moment, your sense of "I" appears to have its own concrete entity, which is neither mind nor body but something that appears much more strongly, does it not?

Or, remember a time when you did something wonderful or something really nice happened to you, and you took great pride in it. This "I" that was so valued, so cherished, so liked, and was the object of such self-importance was so concretely and vividly clear.

At such times, your sense of "I" is particularly obvious. Once you catch hold of such a blatant manifestation of "I," you can cause this strong sense of "I" to appear to your mind, and without letting the way it seems diminish in strength, you can examine, as if from a corner, whether it actually exists in the solid way it appears.

Even in sense perception, phenomena falsely appear to be solid and concrete due to faults in our minds, and because of this false appearance, we are automatically drawn into conceiving that phenomena exist from their own side, in their own right, much like assenting to false appearances in dreams. An unfounded appearance is taken to be true, and then we add many other attributes through improper, counterproductive thinking, creating a mess of afflictive emotions.

Up till now, self-cherishing and its partner, ignorance, have taken up residence in the center of your heart. Despite drawing you into all sorts of actions in an attempt to bring you happiness, these attitudes have created many problems. You need to view self-centeredness as faulty from the depths of your being. Now it is time to leave self-cherishing behind and take up cherishing others, to leave ignorance behind and take up the wisdom that realizes selflessness.

Progress to Enlightenment

Contemplating the meaning of emptiness in this way, you gradually make progress over the paths. The progression is indicated in the mantra in the *Heart of Wisdom Sutra*:

TADYATHA GATE GATE PARAGATE PARASAM-GATE BODHI SVAHA. This Sanskrit mantra trans-lates as, "It is thus: Proceed, proceed, proceed beyond, thoroughly proceed beyond, be founded in enlightenment."

Who is proceeding? It is the "I" that is designated in dependence upon the continuum of the mind. From what are you proceeding? You are moving away from cyclic existence, that state of being under the influence of contaminated actions and counterproductive emotions. To what are you proceeding? You are proceeding to buddhahood that is endowed with a truth body, forever free of suffering and the sources of suffering (afflictive emotions), as well as the predispositions established by afflictive emotions. Upon what causes and condition do you depend as you proceed? You are proceeding in dependence on a path that is a union of compassion and wisdom.

Buddha is telling trainees to go to the other shore. From the viewpoint of the trainee, cyclic existence is on the near side, it is close at hand. On the far shore, a distant place, is nirvana — the state of having passed beyond suffering.

When Buddha says, "TADYATHA GATE GATE PARA-GATE PARASAMGATE BODHI SVAHA," he is telling trainees to proceed over the five paths:

GATE — the path of accumulation
GATE — the path of preparation
PARAGATE — the path of seeing
PARASAMGATE — the path of meditation
BODHI SVAHA — the path of no more learning

Let us identify the nature of spiritual advancement over these five paths:

1. What is the initial path, the *path of accumulation*? It is that period when you mainly practice other-directed motivation and thereby accumulate great stores of merit. Also, although you are practicing a union of motivation and wisdom, your realization of emptiness has not reached the level where stabilizing meditation and analytical meditation are mutually supportive, called "a state arisen from meditation." On this path, you achieve powerfully concentrated meditation, and are working toward a state arisen from meditation realizing emptiness. During this and the following path, you ascertain emptiness in the manner of a dualistic appearance of wisdom and the emptiness being realized.

2. At the point at which you achieve a state of wisdom arisen from meditation realizing emptiness, you pass to the *path of preparation*. By becoming more and more familiar with this state, together with cultivating compassionate motivation, you gradually perceive the appearance of emptiness more clearly over the four levels of the path of preparation (heat, peak, forbearance, and highest mundane qualities).

3. Eventually emptiness is realized directly, without even subtle contamination from dualistic appearance, which has vanished. This is the beginning of the *path of seeing* — the path of initial direct realization of the truth concerning the deep nature of phenomena, passing beyond the mundane level to the supramundane level of the path of seeing in which dualistic appearance has vanished. At this point in the Great Vehicle, the ten bodhisattva levels (called "grounds" because on them special spiritual qualities are engendered, like plants growing on the earth) begin. During the path of seeing and the path of meditation, two types of obstructions, intellectually acquired and innate, are, respectively, overcome. Intellectually acquired states of mind come about through adherence to false systems. For example, there are followers of some Buddhist schools who believe that phenomena conventionally exist by way of their own character, based on the unfounded "reasoning" that if

phenomena were not established in this way, they could not function. This kind of misconception, polluted by an invalid system of tenets, is called artificial, or intellectually acquired. Even if you have accumulated no new predispositions through wrong conceptual thinking in this lifetime, everyone has in their mental continuum predispositions established by adhering to wrong views in former lifetimes. By contrast, innate faulty states of mind have existed in all sentient beings — from insects to humans — since beginningless time and operate of their own accord without depending on faulty scripture and reasoning.

4. Intellectually acquired, or artificial, obstructions are removed through the path of seeing, whereas innate obstructions are more difficult to overcome because you have been conditioned to these faulty states of mind since beginningless time. They must be removed by continued meditation on the meaning of emptiness that was first directly seen on the path of seeing. Because such meditation must take place repeatedly over a long period of time, this phase of the path is called the *path of meditation*. Indeed, you have meditated on emptiness earlier, but the path of meditation refers to a path of extended familiarization.

On this level you pass through the remaining nine bodhisattva grounds. From among the ten grounds, the first seven are called impure, the last three are called pure. This is because on the first seven grounds, you are still in the process of removing afflictive obstructions, and thus through the first part of the eighth ground, you are removing afflictive emotions. The balance of the eighth and then the ninth and the tenth grounds enable you to overcome the obstructions to omniscience.

5. Now, through using the diamond-like concentrated meditation achieved at the end of the ten bodhisattva grounds — the culmination of still having obstructions yet to be overcome — you can effectively undermine the very subtle obstacles to omniscience. The next moment of your mind becomes an omniscient consciousness, and simultaneously the deep nature of the mind becomes the nature body of a buddha. This is the fifth and final path, the *path of no more learning*. From the very subtle wind, or energy — which is one entity with that mind — various pure and impure physical forms spontaneously spring forth to assist sentient beings; these are called the form bodies of a buddha. This is buddhahood, a state of being a source of help and happiness for all sentient beings.

That is a brief explanation of emptiness, the object with respect to which a practitioner first develops the wisdom arisen from hearing, then ascertains it with the wisdom arisen from thinking, and finally in dependence, upon meditation on it, proceeds over the stages of the path. Thus, in order to develop wisdom to higher and higher states, it is necessary to train. Still, due to training in past lifetimes, there are various levels of wisdom that people bring into this lifetime.

Qualities of Buddhahood

A buddha's qualities are described as different "bodies," which can be divided into two general types:

- the truth body, or body of attributes, for the fulfillment of your own welfare
- the form bodies, for the fulfillment of others' welfare

Form bodies, in turn, can be divided by how they appear to beings on different levels of purity and impurity. Highly advanced trainees can access the complete enjoyment body, while other levels of trainees experience a wide variety of emanation bodies. The truth body can also be divided into two types: the nature body and the pristine wisdom truth body. The nature body can be further subdivided into a state of natural purification and a state of adventitious, or caused, purification.

Buddhahood is achieved through the unified cultivation of both motivation and wisdom, which nevertheless have their own respective imprints on buddhahood. The result of cultivating an altruistic motivation is the form bodies of a buddha, which exist for the sake of fulfilling the well-being of others. The imprint of cultivating wisdom is the truth body of a buddha, which is the fulfillment of your own development.

What are the main forms of motivation and wisdom? The primary motivation is an other-directed intention to become enlightened, inspired by love and compassion and inspiring the practice of compassionate deeds, such as giving, morality, and patience. The main form of wisdom is an intelligent consciousness realizing the emptiness of inherent existence.

The result of these is that a buddha is capable of appearing spontaneously without exertion in whatever way is appropriate. The form of these appearances is shaped by the needs of others, not for the sake of that buddha. From a buddha's own viewpoint, buddhahood has the total self-fulfillment of the truth body, in which he or she remains forever.

The exalted qualities of the fruit of the path, buddhahood, such as the ten powers and the four fearlessnesses, are all present in substance in the diamond mind; their manifestation is prevented only by the presence of unfavorable conditions. Buddhahood is manifestly endowed with the ten powers:

1. Knowledge of cause and effect, both impure and pure
2. Knowledge of the fruition of actions
3. Knowledge of high and low—that is, to know those who are superior and those who are inferior, or those who have faith and those having heavy afflictions, and so forth
4. Knowledge of the varieties of dispositions
5. Knowledge of the varieties of trainees' interests in the various techniques of training
6. Knowledge of the paths proceeding to the types of cyclic existence and the paths proceeding to the types of enlightenment
7. Knowledge of the varieties of meditative states and knowledge of others' afflictions as well as states without contamination
8. Knowledge mindful of one's own and others' former lives
9. Knowledge of one's own and others' deaths and births
10. Knowledge of the extinction of all contaminations

And similarly buddhahood is endowed with the four fearlessnesses:

1. Fearlessness with respect to the assertion that I am completely and perfectly enlightened with respect to all phenomena
2. Fearlessness to teach that the afflictions of lust, hatred, and ignorance are obstacles to liberation and that the false appearance is an obstacle to simultaneous cognition of all phenomena, and that, therefore, these are to be ceased
3. Fearlessness to teach the paths of liberation
4. Fearlessness to assert that one has extinguished the contaminations

Since we are endowed in substance with such qualities, it is said that we are enlightened from the very beginning, endowed with a completely good basic mind.

That is a short account of the general Buddhist path. Now let us turn to the inspired poem and its special advice.

PART TWO

Introduction to the Great Completeness

· 5 ·

The Fundamental Principle
Common to All Orders
of Tibetan Buddhism

I HAVE GREAT interest in the statement by many wise persons in all the orders of Tibetan Buddhism that their systems come down to the same final principle, and I feel that this is what I should and must explain. Such an exploration may be controversial, but in any case these great scholar-yogis say that all these systems come down to the same final basic insight, the same principle, because there is indeed a final basic experience on which they all alight. There is no way they would say this just to be polite.

Once there must be such a place of coming together, what is it? I have great interest in pursuing this, looking into this fundamental place of understanding and experience. Each of these systems uses different terminology that has its own special potency in helping people to understand specific points, but when we encounter the varying terminology, we have to consider the context, the special meaning, and the intended referents of those particular terms within those systems without losing sight of the basic principle.

In texts we inherited from India, the basic principle is sometimes called the "fundamental innate mind of clear light" and the "fundamental innate wisdom of clear light"— these two terms having the same meaning. In other texts, it is called the "space-diamond pervading space," whereas in even others it is called the "jewel mind," as, for example, when it is said, "Separate from the jewel mind, there is no buddha and no sentient being."

Then, in Tibet, in some texts, it is called "ordinary consciousness" and "innermost awareness." These terms are used in the context of speaking about freedom from thought, which is psychologically and experientially described as "self-release," "naked release," and "unimpeded penetration"; we will be discussing these in detail later. The innermost awareness is said to be the basis of the appearance of all of the round of suffering (called "cyclic existence") and also the basis of liberation (called "nirvana"). Everything, without exception, is complete in the continuum of innermost awareness. It is even said to be "naturally arisen," since it has always been and always will be.

All of the phenomena of cyclic existence and nirvana

are, when you come down to it, not newly produced by causes and conditions but integrally complete within the nature of primordial naturally arisen innermost awareness; everything is contained within its sphere, within its scope. On the low end, the basis of the dawning of all of the phenomena of the world of suffering is this diamond mind of clear light, and also on the high end, the basis of the dawning of all the pure phenomena of liberation is just this innermost awareness, also called the "diamond mind of clear light."

This is a topic well worth exploring for the sake of furthering our inner peace by opening our minds beyond our usual stream of thoughts; we should look into this with the aim of creating more peace with our neighbors and throughout our world.

Innermost Awareness Pervades Every Type of Consciousness

No matter what kind of consciousness we might consider, the clear light of innermost awareness pervades it. Ice, even when it is solid and very hard, does not pass beyond the nature of water. In the same way, no matter how gross, tough, or coarse conceptions might be, the place from which they dawn and the place into which they vanish when we no longer think them does not pass beyond innermost awareness.

Conceptual awareness appears *from within* the sphere of innermost awareness and finally dissolves *into* the sphere of innermost awareness. Since this is the case, as the early twentieth-century scholar-yogi of the Old Translation School (Tib. Nyingma) Dodrubchen Jigme Tenpe Nyima says, just as oil pervades the entirety of sesame seeds, so clear light pervades all consciousness. He concludes that therefore even at the time of the manifestation of the coarser levels of mind — both during thinking and during the operation of the sensory consciousnesses associated with the eye, ear, nose, tongue, and body — it is possible to identify, through the force of a lama's (a guru's) empowering blessings and quintessential instructions, a subtle feature of clear light that pervades each of these consciousnesses.

Practicing the Path Right Now

How can we take innermost awareness into the spiritual path right now? It is through being introduced to and identifying — in experience — the clear light that pervades all types of consciousnesses and one-pointedly meditating on this, sustaining attention to it within nonthought, nonconceptualization.

Then, as the clear light becomes more and more profound, the types of coarse thoughts diminish more and more. This is why this practice is called "the essential

path through knowledge of which all states are released."
Coming to know this single innermost awareness in our
own experience, we are liberated from all sorts of tense
situations.

To identify innermost awareness, the most difficult
part is to make the distinction between mind (Tib.
sems) and innermost awareness (Tib. *rig pa*). It is easy
to talk about this difference from our mouth, to say
"Innermost awareness has never been infected by mistake, whereas mind is under the influence of conceptu-
alization and polluted with mistaken thought." This is
easy to say, but in terms of actual experience in our own
mental continuum, it is very difficult. Dodrubchen said
that although we might fancy that we are meditating on
innermost awareness, there is a danger that we are actually, in fact, merely maintaining concentration on the
clear and cognitive nature of a more superficial mind,
and so we need to take care. It is helpful to do the latter
but it is not so profound.

Here in this book, we will explore how to place oneself in the core of innermost awareness by examining a
Tibetan text of the Old Translation School of Tibetan
Buddhism. You may find it psychologically and spiritu-
ally thrilling.

· 6 ·

The Innate Mind of Clear Light

THE OLD Translation School of Tibetan Buddhism presents a series of styles of practice called "vehicles." Among these, the vehicle of the Great Completeness is the peak of peaks of all vehicles, while the others are said to be systems wrought in terms of lower levels of practice. By way of the division between mind and innermost awareness that I just mentioned, these lower systems are practiced through mind, whereas in the ninth vehicle, the Great Completeness, innermost awareness is used as the spiritual path.

No Exertion

Primordially, in all of us is self-sustaining innermost awareness. Abiding within, it is to be introduced and brought out in all its nakedness and implemented as the spiritual path itself. Since it is practiced as the path, this system is called a "Vehicle Free from Exertion."

Such terminology has its own special potency and bestows understanding with a particular purpose. When it is called a vehicle *without exertion*, this does not mean not doing anything at all. It would not be suitable just to remain lying down and eating! Rather, this vocabulary contains a profound essential, calling for meditation solely within taking innermost awareness as the path. In the beginning stages of practice in other systems, there are many practices involving conceptuality even though eventually the nonconceptual mind of clear light is manifested, whereas right from the very beginning, in the Great Completeness conceptuality is not stressed and emphasis is placed on innermost awareness in reliance upon special quintessential instructions. This is why it is called a doctrine free from exertion.

The Centrality of the Mind of Clear Light

In fact, all Tibetan systems, in their final view, emphasize the fundamental innate mind of clear light. In terms of the center of these systems, all of the phenomena of cyclic existence and nirvana are the sport, the effulgence, of the fundamental innate clear light. Hence, the root, and foundation, of all of that is within the scope of cyclic existence and nirvana is the fundamental clear light. This being so, when practicing the spiritual path, there is nothing else needed to purify these impure appearances — that themselves dawn from within the context of innermost awareness or clear light — than to turn the fundamental innate mind of clear light itself into that through which you practice the spiritual path. Also, when finally manifesting the fruit of practicing the path, the fundamental innate mind of clear light itself, when separated from all obstructive defilements, is the resultant omniscience of buddhahood, a state from which the greatest benefit to others can be effected.

Types of Books

It is important to understand that there is no such thing as a division of Buddhist doctrines into ones for explanation and others for practice. You might think that since long complicated texts set forth doctrines that are not, at your present level, applicable to your daily practice, such books are meant to provide philosophical explanations merely for debate with others, whereas other, shorter texts provide what is to be practiced. This would be a great mistake. You need to understand that all of the Buddha's scriptures and their commentaries are necessary for enlightenment, and you need to know how to take all of them as guidance for implementation in practice, now or later. It would be ridiculous to study one thing and then practice something else. At a minimum, the more complicated teachings provide a map for spiritual progress that itself will influence your journey; they are your road map. Nevertheless, there are teachings that mainly emphasize the stages of practice and others that mainly emphasize making detailed conclusions. Then again, the great Indian adepts' songs of insight especially contain practical experience involving high spiritual paths and are mainly in a style presenting the direct, spontaneous mode of those yogis' experience. In these cases, gurus who have reached a deep level of spiritual development express their realizations for appropriate students.

Also, many scholar-yogis in all of the Tibetan orders have texts that mainly present their experiences in song. I will now explain the text *Three Keys Penetrating the Core*, which is among those that spontaneously set forth meditative experience; it is from the mind of the great adept Dza Patrul Jigme Chokyi Wangpo (1808–87). He was a great scholar-yogi, an inconceivable person. He himself assumed a low bearing. There is an account that says that many students came to live in his quarters to be near him and receive his teaching, and at one point, in order to get away, to escape to a quiet place, he went to another area, where he was taken on as a servant by a woman who owned a rest house; she had no idea who he was. He worked hard at his duties, sweeping the floor and performing other chores, including emptying the nightly urine pots in the morning.

Several of his students came to that area looking for their great teacher, asking those whom they met if their lama was staying anywhere in the vicinity, eventually encountering this woman. They asked her if she had seen Dza Patrul Rinpoche, and she said she had not, but she asked for a description of him, which they provided. She replied, "Someone wearing old raggedy clothes came, and I made him my servant." The students knew immediately that it was he, and upon the lady's learning that this great adept and scholar was living in her house as her lowly servant, she ran away in embarrassment.

PART THREE

*Commentary on
Patrul Rinpoche's* Three Keys
Penetrating the Core

Dza Patrul Jigme Chokyi Wangpo

Drawing courtesy of Chris Banigan

The First Key

Introducing Innermost Awareness

PATRUL RINPOCHE's teaching, and thus his poem, is organized around three keys for uncovering innermost awareness, the Great Completeness. The essential meaning of how to place yourself in the core of reality is cast into three sets of quintessential teachings for the sake of severing the life, so to speak, of self-ruinous mistake. Let us start with the first key; his poem says:

The view, the multitudinous expanse,
Is cast in practical essentials of three keys.

I.

First set your own mind in a relaxed state,
Not emitting, not withdrawing, without
    conceptuality.
In this relaxed state of total absorption,

Suddenly shout PAṬ, striking your awareness,
Strong, intense, short. E MA HO!
Not any thing, astounding.
Astounding, unimpeded penetration.
Unimpeded penetration, inexpressible.
Identify innermost awareness of the truth body.
Its entity is identified within yourself—the first
  essential.

I will try to provide a little commentary.

Relax

The initial introduction to the view of naturally arisen innermost awareness cannot be made while you are involved in constantly generating many conceptions, such as thinking about good and bad and the like. For instance, it is difficult to be introduced to and identify somebody in a huge crowd, but once you have been introduced to a person and come to know him or her, it is easy to identify the person even in the midst of a big crowd. Similarly, even though innermost awareness pervades every moment of consciousness, including every single thought, it is not possible to bring out innermost awareness in its nakedness without being introduced to it first, because it is bound and obscured by conceptual thinking. However, after you have identified it, you can see it even in the midst of a multitude of thoughts.

Therefore, without making any adjustments to your mind, such as by conceptually working at analysis, leave, among the various phenomena of the world, whatever appears to your mind — people, buildings, mountains, your work, your friends, your problems, and the like — as just an appearance, and do not get involved and polluted with identifying it and thinking about it, "This is such-and-such." Since a state of mere appearance and mere awareness needs to be sustained, do as the author of the poem says and "**first set your own mind in a relaxed state**," not allowing the busy state of a multitude of thoughts.

Stop Thinking for a While

Naturally arisen innermost awareness naturally exists within you; it is naturally there, not newly generated or constructed by superficial conditions. Rather, it is original wisdom, naturally flowing awareness whose continuum is itself fundamental, uncontrived. For it to become evident to you now, do not allow new superficially fabricated conceptions to develop. Do not emit new thoughts, but even when you notice that conceptions have been produced, do not make the exertion of thinking that they have to be withdrawn; just let them disappear: as the poem says, "**not emitting, not withdrawing, without conceptuality.**" Rather, vividly stay completely within the self-flow, the natural flow of nonconceptuality; on the spot, let go of all conceptual thinking altogether.

For example, if a number of people are going along as a group, and a couple of them stop but the others go on, they have not stopped together, but if they all stop simultaneously, they have completely stopped altogether.

Shock

Still, it is not sufficient just to keep your mind from diffusing and scattering. Even if bliss, clarity, and nonconceptuality dawn in meditative experience, these interfere with being introduced to and identifying naturally arisen innermost awareness. You need to avoid even bliss, clarity, and nonconceptuality. You have to get beyond all of these.

Therefore, in this relaxed state not affected and polluted by the tightness of conceptuality, suddenly shout PAṬ (pronounced "pat," with the tongue curled to the top of the mouth behind the front teeth while saying the final "t"), strong, intense, and short, for the sake of immediately clearing out any and all of the commotion of thinking "It is so-and-so," "It is like this," "It is like that." The sudden sound of PAṬ will strike conceptual thinking out of your consciousness: "**In this relaxed state of total absorption, suddenly shout PAṬ, striking your awareness, strong, intense, short. E MA HO! Not any thing, astounding.**"

Old thoughts have stopped and new thoughts have not yet been produced. For example, when a boat moves quickly through water, the water is moved to the two sides with an empty place right then and there in its wake at the back of the boat.

At the point of shouting PAṬ, between when you are unable to emit earlier conceptions—that is, unable to think your former thoughts—and before you are able to produce new conceptions, in between those two, when you cannot make conceptual distinctions, there is astonishment, clarity, vividness, mere knowing.

If you have faith and keen interest, as well as a guide's quintessential instructions, then remaining in place of the sudden removal of thoughts will be a sense of shock that cannot be identified as anything, this or that. The clothing of thought suddenly thrown off, you will be left in a state of wonder, feeling astounded, astonished.

There are several types of shock. One is like having your eyes closed in which you cannot think anything; another is a state of nonconceptuality in which the mind is free from the pollutions of the mind being either too loose or too tight. There are also others. At this juncture, the emitting and withdrawing of conceptuality has stopped to the point where you are in a state of astonishment, having lost the power of recognizing objects as this or that.

With a shock, mental activity suddenly halts. For example, when a dog suddenly barks near you, you can be shocked into being unable to think anything, aghast. Here, in this practice, you are released from the varieties of thought, from the binding confines of the groups of adventitiously generated new conceptions, but still you are not as if having fainted. Rather, the perspective of your consciousness is vividly clear.

Texts speak of making evident a state in which the usual underlying consciousness has lost its intensity and conceptual apprehension cannot get started, and thus during this interval naked innermost awareness can manifest for a period. The great Tibetan scholar Mangto Lhundrub Gyatsho cites many scriptural sources such as:

> Between earlier and later conceptions, the contin-uum of the clear light of innermost awareness re-mains unbroken.

In the space between two thoughts, there is an easy opportunity for identifying this moment of innermost awareness.

Therefore, this state of shock is not just astonishment, but also has unimpeded penetration, so the author of the poem, Patrul Rinpoche, says, "**Astounding, unimpeded penetration.**"

The nature of this is to be known, just as it actually is, in the context of experience, and is otherwise indescribable in words, so he says, "**Unimpeded penetration, inexpressible.**" Though *called* innermost awareness of the truth body, it is inexpressible as any of the poles of being existent, nonexistent, and so forth. This innermost awareness of the truth body must be identified in experience.

Unless you can identify it, there is no way to sustain the view of the Great Completeness in meditation. This type of meditation, in which you are sustaining the experience of innermost awareness, is a case of remaining within the experience of that which you are meditating, rather than meditating *on* an object.

Beyond this, as is clear in Dodrubchen's writings, if you are able to recognize all phenomena as the sport, the vibration, or effervescence of this naturally arisen innermost awareness, this allows you to easily see that all phenomena do not exist in and of themselves, independently, and are only set up by conceptuality. When you identify innermost awareness, also called ultimate truth, and ascertain that all the phenomena of cyclic existence and nirvana are its effulgence, then along the way you understand that all pure and impure phenomena are, as the philosophical texts say, only nominally existent. You understand that all appearing and occurring objects of knowledge are adventitious and essenceless, that although such phenomena have, from the start, not been established under their own power, they nonetheless appear to you to have their own autonomous nature, whereupon you adhere to this sense of seeming existence from their own side. You further understand that this misapprehension leads to engagement in various good and bad actions and the accumulation of those predispositions, leading to still more entanglement in cyclic existence.

To identify innermost awareness and properly sustain it in meditation, it is important to have previously reflected on such procedures as from where the mind arises, where it abides, and that into which it ceases, as well as other analytical techniques. For these practices, the reasonings as are laid out in the great texts are helpful.

If you can cause all these phenomena to appear as the vibration of innermost awareness within not deviating from the sphere of that mind, you will not come under the influence of conventional conceptions. When you identify your own basic entity yourself and directly ascertain its meaning continuously and forever in meditative equipoise, then even though acting in the world, you are enlightened.

· 8 ·

The Supreme Way to Rest

SIMILAR TO THE Old Translation School, in the New
Translation Schools in Tibet it is said that when the
clear light is actualized, the great yogi rests. Let us di-
verge a little and look into this; it will deepen our exploration of the same final principle shared by all the orders
of Tibetan Buddhism, the Old Translation School and
the New Translation Schools.

What is needed on the spiritual path is for all the
varieties of dualistic and conceptual proliferations to
disappear, to vanish, into the sphere of the fundamental
innate mind of clear light. Why? So that you understand
their nature and origin and learn how to appear in physical form for the sake of others. What are these "dualistic
and conceptual proliferations"?

Levels of Consciousness

Many texts describe several different categories of mind
or consciousness, ranging from the gross to the subtle.

The grossest level are the consciousnesses associated with the eyes, ears, nose, tongue, and body. More subtle is the mental consciousness, or what we usually consider the thinking and imagining mind, which itself actually ranges from gross levels, such as ordinary thought, to deep sleep and fainting, when the breath has stopped, to the innermost subtle mind of clear light.

The Buddhist view is that although coarse consciousnesses do have a beginning and an end, there is no beginning to the subtle mind. The subtle mind always remains — continuously, without beginning or end — and thus the cause and effect of karma also have no beginning. Except in extraordinary meditative states, this subtlest, or deepest, consciousness manifests only when we are dying, although less withdrawn and therefore brief versions of the subtle levels of consciousness also occur when going to sleep, ending a dream, sneezing, yawning, and during orgasm. When the mind of the clear light of death finally manifests, all of the multiplying proliferations of ordinary life vanish into it.

The process of dying provides a powerful way to examine the levels of mind, so let us consider it in some detail. Dying occurs in stages, involving a serial dissolution, or cessation, of the four internal elements:

- earth, the capacity of the hard substances of the body to support consciousness

- water, the capacity of the fluids of the body to support consciousness
- fire, the capacity of the heat of the body to support consciousness
- wind, the capacity of the motile energy of the body to support consciousness

In ordinary life, these elements serve as the mount, or basis, for consciousness; these elements are like a horse, and consciousness is like a rider on the horse. During the process of dying, the capacity of these elements to support consciousness decreases, beginning with the hard elements of the body, when their capacity to support consciousness shifts over, so to speak, to the fluid elements of the body. Each step in this dissolution thereby increases the capacity of the next element to serve as a foundation for consciousness.

EIGHT STAGES OF DYING

Step by step it looks like this:

1. The capacity of the earth element (the hard substances of your body such as bone) to support consciousness dissolves into the water element (the fluids of your body such as blood and phlegm). The external indication of this is that your body becomes thinner; internally, you see what appears to be a mirage as seen in a desert or on a hot highway in the distance.

2. Then the capacity of the fluids of your body to support consciousness dissolves into the fire element (the heat of your body). The external signs of this are that your fluids dry—your mouth becomes waterless, your nose puckers, and other fluids, such as urine, blood, regenerative fluid, and sweat, dry up; internally, you see what is variously described as puffs of smoke from a chimney or smoke floating throughout a room.

3. Then the capacity of the heat of your body to support consciousness dissolves into the wind element (the currents of energy that direct various bodily functions such as inhalation, exhalation, burping, spitting, speaking, swallowing, flexing the joints, stretching and contracting the limbs, opening and closing the mouth and eyelids, digestion, urination, defecation, menstruation, and ejaculation). The external indication of this is that your bodily heat diminishes, resulting in an inability to digest food; breathing is difficult, exhalations become longer and longer and inhalations shorter and shorter; and your throat emits rattling or gasping sounds. Internally, you see what look like fireflies at night or like sparks in the soot on the bottom of a metal pan in a campfire; sometimes these are described as like sparks inside of smoke.

4. Then the movement of energy in your body dissolves, and breathing through the nostrils ceases. At this time,

you see an appearance like the light above a flickering butter lamp or candle flame when the fuel has almost been used up. Then the flickering light is followed by the appearance of a steady flame.

The next and final four phases of dying require that the conceptual level of consciousness dissolves. These conceptual consciousnesses are more subtle than the five sense consciousnesses but are still on the gross level of mind. They are grouped into three classes, corresponding to three types of winds, or energies, on which they ride — strong, middling, and weak.

- The first group is composed of conceptual consciousnesses that involve a strong movement of the energy of consciousness to its objects and includes thirty-three conceptual experiences such as fear, attachment, hunger, thirst, compassion, acquisitiveness, and jealousy.
- The second group is composed of conceptual consciousnesses that involve a medium movement of the energy of consciousness to its objects and includes forty conceptual experiences such as joy, amazement, generosity, desiring to kiss, heroism, nongentleness, and crookedness.
- The third group is composed of conceptual consciousnesses that involve a weak movement of energy to its objects and includes seven conceptual experiences, which are forgetfulness; mistake, as in apprehending

water in a mirage; catatonia; depression; laziness; doubt; and equally desire and hatred.

These three categories of conceptual experiences are reflections of deeper levels of consciousness that have less and less dualistic perception since they are imprints of three subtle levels of mind that manifest at times when the grosser levels of consciousness cease, either intentionally, as in profound states of meditation, or naturally, as in the process of dying or in going to sleep.

When the energies on which all eighty of these conceptual experiences ride — like a rider on a horse — dissolve, the basis of consciousness shifts from grosser to subtler levels of energy (which Buddhists call "subtle wind"), allowing three *subtle levels* of consciousness to manifest. As you proceed through these three levels, your consciousness becomes increasingly nondualistic with less and less sense of subject and object. These lead finally to the *very subtle level* of consciousness, the mind of clear light, which, if utilized in the spiritual path, is most powerful. Here are these final, four deep levels:

5. When the energies that serve as the mounts, like a horse, of the many types of conceptual consciousnesses, like a rider, dissolve, your mind itself turns into an omnipresent, huge, vivid white vastness. It is described as being like a clear sky filled with moonlight — not the

moon shining in empty space but empty space filled with white light. Conceptual thought has vanished, and nothing appears except this vivid whiteness, which is your consciousness. However, a subtle sense of subject and object remains, so the state is slightly dualistic. This is called the "mind of vivid white appearance" because an appearance like moonlight dawns, and it is also called "empty" because it is beyond those conceptual consciousnesses and the energies (winds) on which they ride.

6. When the mind of white appearance and its energies dissolve, your mind turns into a red or orange vastness, more vivid than before; nothing else appears. It is like a clear sky filled with sunlight — not the sun shining in the sky but space itself filled with red or orange light. In this state, the mind is even less dualistic. It is called the "mind of increase-of-appearance" because an appearance like very vivid sunlight appears, and it is also called "very empty" because it is beyond the former mind of appearance and the energies on which that mind rides.

7. When the mind of red or orange increase-of-appearance and its energies dissolve, your mind itself turns into a still more subtle, vividly black state; nothing else appears. This is called the "mind of near-attainment" because you are close to manifesting the mind of clear

light. The mind of black vastness is like a moonless, very dark sky just after dusk when no stars are seen. During the first phase of the mind of black near-attainment, you are still aware, but in the latter phase, you become unconscious in a very thick darkness, like when you faint. This stage is called "near-attainment" because it is close to manifestation of the mind of clear light, and it is also called "greatly empty" because it is beyond the earlier mind of increase-of-appearance and the energies on which it rides.

8. When the mind of black near-attainment dissolves, the swoon of unconsciousness is cleared away, and your mind itself turns into the mind of clear light. Called the "fundamental innate mind of clear light," this is the most subtle, profound, and powerful level of consciousness. Totally nonconceptual and nondualistic, it is like the sky's natural state at dawn (long before sunrise) — without moonlight, sunlight, or darkness. This deepest level is called the "fundamental innate mind of clear light" because it is not temporary, whereas the minds of black near-attainment, red-orange increase-of-appearance, white appearance, and so on are *newly* produced and bound to cease through the power of conditions, and thus are temporary and adventitious. The mind of clear light is also called "all-empty" because it is beyond the entire scope of conceptual consciousness

as well as the three subtle minds of white, red/orange, and black appearances.

To repeat: When the actual process of dying begins, you pass through eight phases — the first four involve the collapse of the four elements, and the last four involve the collapse of consciousness into the innermost level of mind, called the mind of clear light.

The passage through to the mind of clear light can be fast or slow. Some people remain in the final stage, the mind of clear light of death, for only several minutes; others stay for as long as a week or two. For a capable practitioner, this is a valuable opportunity for practice. Those who are conscious of the mind of clear light can remain in this state for longer periods and, depending on previous training, can even use it to realize the truth of the emptiness of the inherent existence of all phenomena.

Some of my meditator friends have reported deep experiences of dissolution, but still within the realm of *similitudes* of the actual ones. Several Tibetans, declared to be clinically dead, have remained without undergoing physical decomposition for quite some time. Recently, the body of a lama from the Sakya order remained fresh without decomposing for more than twenty days. He "died" in Dharamsala, India, but he remained, while still here in Dharamsala, in meditation; then his body was carried to Rajpur in the Dehra Dun area, where it still remained fresh. It was remarkable. I know of about fifteen Tibetans whose bodies similarly stayed without decomposition — some for a few days, some longer, the maximum being three weeks. My own senior tutor, Ling Rinpoche, remained for thirteen days.

The cornerstone of my own practice is reflection on the four basic teachings of impermanence, suffering, emptiness, and selflessness, and in addition, as a part of eight different daily ritual practices, I meditate on the stages of dying. I imagine the dissolution of the earth element into water, the water element into fire, and so forth — all eight phases. Though I cannot claim any profound experience, there is a little stoppage of breath when the ritual calls for imagining the dissolving of all appearances. I am sure more complete versions manifest if a practitioner visualizes the dissolutions in a more leisurely and thorough way. Since my daily practices of imagining myself in ideal mental and physical form, called deity yoga, all involve visualizing death, I am habituating myself to the process, and thus, at the actual time of death, these steps will likely be familiar. But whether I will succeed or not, I do not know.

In the final phase of dying, when all coarse consciousnesses dissolve into the all-empty, which is the fundamental innate mind of clear light, the myriad objects of the world, as well as concepts such as sameness and difference, are pacified in this subtlest mind. At that time, all appearances of environments and beings withdraw of their own accord. Even for a nonpractitioner, coarse appearances also withdraw; this withdrawal of conventional appearances, however, is not due to a perception of reality attained through meditation. When, in the last phase, the temporary winds that carry consciousness have all dissolved, the mind (whether of a practitioner or a nonpractitioner) becomes as if undifferentiated, and an immaculate openness dawns.

USING THE DEEPEST LEVEL OF MIND IN THE SPIRITUAL PATH

As a practitioner, however, you seek to go beyond this ordinary emptiness, this mere absence of conventional appearances. When the clear light dawns, you seek to realize the extraordinary emptiness of inherent existence with the mind of clear light itself. This will not come about through exertion at the time of the clear light, but it arises from the force of familiarity gained prior to the phases of dissolution and from the strong mindfulness of emptiness during the dawning of the three minds of white, red/orange, and black appearance. If you are able to transform the clear light of death into a fully qualified spiritual consciousness, the mind recognizes its own face, its own nature—the entity of the fundamental mind.

This is how subtler states of mind are utilized in more powerful and effective ways when used in spiritual practice. This shows the importance of continual training. The presentation of the phases of death is a mapping of deeper states of mind that occur throughout daily life and usually go unnoticed and unutilized.

These eight phases proceed in forward order not only when dying but also when going to sleep, ending a dream, sneezing, fainting, and during orgasm, and in reverse order not only after the process of death completely ends but also when waking from sleep and when beginning a dream as well as at the end of sneezing, fainting, and orgasm.

FORWARD ORDER

1. Appearance of mirage
2. Appearance of smoke
3. Appearance of fireflies
4. Appearance of the flame of a lamp
5. Mind of vivid white appearance
6. Mind of vivid red/orange increase-of-appearance
7. Mind of vivid black near-attainment
8. Mind of clear light

REVERSE ORDER

8. Mind of clear light
7. Mind of vivid black near-attainment

6. Mind of vivid red/orange increase-of-appearance
5. Mind of vivid white appearance
4. Appearance of the flame of a lamp
3. Appearance of fireflies
2. Appearance of smoke
1. Appearance of mirage

In the forward process, the coarser levels of consciousness — our five sense consciousnesses, as well as our thinking mind and the three subtle levels of consciousness — finally dissolve into the fundamental innate mind of clear light. It is called the "all-empty" because it is devoid of all these coarser levels. It is very powerful, but when these coarser levels of consciousness naturally dissolve — as they do, for instance, at death — we have no ability to remain in the mind of clear light, and due to this, after that period of dissolution, the reverse process begins, and the phenomena of dualistic and conceptual proliferation reappear. These two series, a forward process of dissolution and a reverse process of devolution, hinge on the fundamental innate mind of clear light. (For more on the levels of consciousness, see His Holiness the Dalai Lama, *Mind of Clear Light: Advice on Living Well and Dying Consciously* [New York: Atria Books, 2003].)

In the vocabulary of the New Translation Schools of Tibet, all the conceptual proliferations causing actions that result in the accumulation of predispositions are consciousnesses more coarse than even the minds of appearance, increase, and near-attainment that must cease before the mind of clear light can dawn. Having manifested the mind of clear light, if we are unable to remain in it, the minds of near-attainment, increase, and appearance will be generated, and the eighty conceptions will arise, from which contaminated actions will once again occur, and their predispositions will accumulate. This is what causes harm. However, when the eighty conceptual consciousnesses as well as the three minds of appearance, increase, and near-attainment cease and we steadily abide in the clear light, conceptions and afflictive emotions cannot be generated. Remaining within this state, we are beyond the scope of conceptuality; not even the strongest of afflictive emotions can intrude at this stage. It is a real rest.

The Clear Light within All Consciousnesses

That is the presentation of the New Translation Schools. However, profound, distinctive features of the Great Completeness stem from the presence of clear light in all consciousnesses. Without having to wait to utilize the fundamental innate mind of clear light on the path until after all of the coarse and subtle levels of wind-energy and consciousness have ceased through meditative techniques, if we come to understand the reality of the diamond mind, this mode of reality, within manifestation of the six types of consciousnesses, we understand all appearances of cyclic existence and nirvana as arising through its force, as its sport, through which we realize that these phenomena do not exist in their own right but through the force of this basic mind, innermost awareness. Just as in Nagarjuna's *Precious Garland*, cyclic existence is shown to be false because it arises in dependence on a false cause, ignorance, so although innermost awareness is, of course, not itself false, since the phenomena of cyclic existence and nirvana are the sport of innermost awareness yet do not appear as such, from this viewpoint, all these phenomena are shown to be false. Through realizing this, we perforce understand that these phenomena exist only nominally. Dodrubchen says that when we are able to ascertain all appearing and occurring objects of knowledge as the sport of innermost awareness, we perforce understand even better the philosophical position that these exist only through the power of conceptuality.

The Great Completeness presents a practice of viewing all phenomena of cyclic existence and nirvana as the sport and the self-effulgence of the mind within sustaining awareness of the basic entity of the mind. Even though there is little explanation of the negation of inherent existence by reasoning and of the realization of phenomena as only nominally designated, these facts are understood as a by-product of understanding that all of these phenomena are just the manifestations, the sport, of clear light, the innermost awareness. Therefore, all of the important essentials of the view of emptiness as found in the New Translation Schools' presentation of the Middle Way School are contained within this practice.

· *9* ·

The All-Good Diamond Mind

IN THE Great Completeness, the naturally arisen clear light is called the "all-good" and "the mind-hero of no beginning and no end." Naturally pure from the start and endowed with a spontaneous nature, this diamond mind is the basis of all the phenomena occurring in cyclic existence and nirvana. Even while you are still a sentient being and despite the generation of a great many good and bad conceptions such as manifest desire, hatred, and bewilderment, the diamond mind itself is free from the pollutions of these defilements. Water may be extremely dirty; yet its nature remains just clear — its nature is not polluted by dirt. Similarly, no matter what afflictive emotions are generated as the sport of this diamond mind and no matter how powerful they are, innermost awareness itself, the basis of the appearance of such vibrancy, remains unaffected by defilement, beginninglessly pure, all-good.

Aiming Your Attention at Space

One of the techniques in the Great Completeness is to aim your consciousness at your eyes and aim your eyes at space. This indeed helps because your eye consciousness is so powerful that it can thereby bring some help even when you are meditating. This is not a matter of looking out into the external world, but of looking into intermediate space; even in the New Translation Schools, it is said that there are similarities between internal empty space and external empty space, and between internal enlightenment and external enlightenment. It is not being said that external space is something extremely fantastic; rather, it symbolizes inner space.

First of all, straighten up your body and keep your mind from being distracted to anything else. Aim your consciousness at your eyes, and aim your eyes at space. Do not allow the factor of conceptual apprehension to pollute your mind at all; vividly set yourself in the entity of essential purity, of luminosity, of innermost awareness.

Identifying Innermost Awareness

Because such a view means identifying innermost awareness in your own experience, you need to remain one-pointedly within it. Except for identifying a nature that integrally exists in you, there is nothing to newly delineate outside of yourself. Since you are to identify, to manifest in experience, and then stay with the reality of this innermost awareness that integrally exists within you yourself, the author of the poem, Patrul Rinpoche, says, "**Identify innermost awareness of the truth body. Its entity is identified within yourself— the first essential.**" This nature has existed in yourself beginninglessly without having to be newly set up; you are identifying what is within yourself now.

Introduction to the view is not at all easy. An experienced lama and a faithful, keen student are needed. Great Completeness teachings say that you cannot become enlightened through a fabricated mind; rather, innermost awareness is to be identified, whereupon all phenomena are to be understood as the sport of that mind. You need to induce continuous one-pointed ascertainment in this.

With such practice, it is not necessary to repeat mantras, recite texts, and so forth, because you have something greater. These other practices are fabricated — they require exertion — whereas when you identify innermost awareness and sustain practice within that, it is a spontaneous practice without exertion. Practices requiring exertion are done by the mind, but spontaneous practices without exertion are done by innermost awareness.

To do this, it is not sufficient merely to read books; you need the full preparatory practice of the Old

Translation School and, in addition, you need the special teachings of a qualified Old Translation School master, as well as his or her blessings. Also, the student must also have accumulated great merit. The great Old Translation School master Jigme Lingpa himself spent three years and three phases of the moon in retreat with tremendous effort after which the sphere of innermost awareness manifested; it did not come easily. Dodrubchen similarly worked very hard; throughout his writings he emphasizes that someone engaging in this spontaneous practice without exertion must work hard at all the preparatory practices, be introduced to innermost awareness by a lama with actual experience, and meditate on it one-pointedly within total renunciation of this life. He says that through this the sphere of innermost awareness can be identified, not otherwise.

10

The Second Key
Maintaining Meditation

Having been introduced to and having identified this view, you need to engage in a continuous mode of meditation. This is the impact of the second key.

11.

Then, whether spreading out or abiding within,
Whether angry or desirous, happy or sad,
At all times and occasions,
Recognize the identified pristine wisdom truth body.
For those with prior acquaintance, the mother and
    child clear lights meet.
Be founded in the inexpressible state of the quality of
    innermost awareness.
Stability, bliss, luminosity, and delight should again
    and again be destroyed.

Make the syllable of method and wisdom suddenly
    descend.
Meditative equipoise and subsequent attainment do
    not differ.
Continuously dwelling in the undifferentiable state,
Session and between-session are not divided.
However, until attaining stability,
Meditation within having abandoned commotion is
    to be valued.
Practice is done within division into sessions.
At all times and occasions,
Maintain the display of just the truth body.
Be firmly decided that there is none other than this.
Be determined on this alone — the second essential.

No Danger

After you have identified the natural face of innermost awareness through ascertaining it in yourself, once it is experienced as underneath you like your own bed, your experiential floor, no matter what sort of conceptuality occurs, whether thoughts spread out or withdraw and cease, it is not necessary to intentionally work at stopping those conceptions. Rather, when good or bad conceptions dawn, whether good things happen or bad things happen, you realize on all occasions that these dawn from within the sphere of this unimpeded, penetrating innermost awareness that you have already identified, and when they cease, they cease into it.

If you are able to successfully remain in recognition of innermost awareness, then even if thoughts arise, no matter what those conceptions are, they pose no danger since they are seen from the perspective of not passing beyond the range of innermost awareness. Without need for analysis, you recognize that any thoughts arise in the context of innermost awareness and dissolve there too. Thus: **"Whether spreading out or abiding within, whether angry or desirous, happy or sad, at all times and occasions, recognize the identified pristine wisdom truth body."**

Clouds and Sky

This being the case, on occasions when many various conceptions are generated, it is not necessary to rely on exertion and apply antidotes to them one by one. Rather, recognize the wisdom truth body that you previously identified, and pay attention to it. As the great Tibetan yogi Milarepa says in song, "Clouds, whether arising, arise from the sky itself, or dissolving, dissolve into the sky itself."

Or, it is like a piece of ice melting into water.

Also, consider this: When water becomes dirty, if you stir it up, it gets more and more dirty, but if you allow water to stay still, gradually it settles down and becomes pure. Similarly, leaving conceptions in their own flow, pay attention to their inner nature and stay within the context of innermost awareness without losing it. By remaining within this, conceptions will contract and diminish.

Meeting of Mother and Child

In our ordinary state, whether we are or are not a meditator, no matter who we are, the naturally arisen innermost awareness has been with us primordially, and for this reason it is called the "mother clear light." This basic clear light, despite being always existent, previously was not identified, but once you are introduced by a lama to the clear light, this new state — now that its existence has been identified — is called the "child clear light."

In this way, we speak of two states of innermost awareness: the primordially existent naturally arisen innermost awareness, the mother clear light, and the identified innermost awareness, the child clear light. The *identification* of the natural face of the naturally arisen innermost awareness that has integrally existed with yourself is called the *meeting* of the mother and child clear lights and also the *mixing* of the mother and child clear lights. Although these are not actually two things, an object met (the mother clear light) and a meeter (the child clear light), or an object mixed (the mother clear light) and a mixer (the child clear light), you have identified what has integrally existed all along in the basic state. This is metaphorically treated as the meeting of the mother and child clear lights. The message of the metaphor is that we need to identify what is already within.

The Clear Light of Death

In the New Translation Schools, they also speak about the meeting of the mother and child clear lights when dying. Earlier, I explained a little about this, but let me add some more detail here. In the ordinary process of dying, when the mind of clear light of death finally dawns, appearances of the world as we know it withdraw of their own accord. In the final four of the eight stages of dying, the winds (or energies) that serve as the mounts on which consciousness rides become increasingly subtle. When, in the last phase, the temporary winds that carry consciousness have all dissolved, the mind (whether of a practitioner or a nonpractitioner) becomes as if undifferentiated, and an immaculate openness naturally dawns through the force of karma.

In this last phase of dying, when all the coarse consciousnesses dissolve into the all-empty, the clear light, the fundamental innate mind, the myriad objects of the world, as well as concepts such as sameness and difference, disappear in this subtlest mind. A practitioner seeks to go beyond this ordinary emptiness, this mere absence of conventional appearances. When the clear light dawns, a practitioner aims to realize *with the mind of clear light itself* the extraordinary emptiness of inherent existence. This will not come about through exertion at the time of the clear light, but it arises from the force of familiarity gained in practical meditation, which through strong mindfulness is maintained during daily life, and then at the end of life prior to and during the phases of dissolution, and finally during the dawning of the three minds of white, red, and black appearance. All of this depends upon having cultivated the spiritual path through exertion in earlier meditation. If you are an accomplished practitioner, you may be able to transform the clear light of death into a fully qualified spiritual consciousness, such that the mind recognizes its own face, its own nature, the entity of the fundamental mind, innermost awareness.

If, through the power of previous training in yoga, you can transform the mind of clear light integrally existing within you in the ordinary state into a spiritual path, this is also called the meeting of the mother and child clear lights or the mixing of the mother and child clear lights. The mind of clear light that is a natural part of you in the ordinary state is called the mother clear light, and the clear light cultivated on the yogic path is called the child clear light. If, at the time of the dawning of the mother clear light at death, you are able to transform it into the spiritual path, this is the meaning — in this context — of the mother and child clear lights meeting or mixing. Again, this is not actually a meeting of two entities; rather, the mother clear light of death, which dawns due to karma, turns into a spiritual consciousness, the child clear light. Due to previous training, the mother clear light does not become an ordinary mind of death but is used to realize the truth of the emptiness of inherent existence, thereby undermining the afflictive emotions built on misapprehending phenomena as existing in and of themselves, independently.

Mother and Child Clear Lights in the Poem

When Patrul Rinpoche says, **"For those with prior acquaintance, the mother and child clear lights meet,"** here the meaning is the first of the two just explained. One clear light, the mother clear light, except for not having been identified, has naturally existed in us; the clear light to which we are introduced by a lama and which we identify and meditatively cultivate is the child clear light. Though the clear light of innermost awareness has always been there, it has not been identified; the mother and child clear lights have not met, so to speak. However, when a lama has introduced us to that which has innately been there and we have identified it through the power of our own intimate experience, this recognition is called the meeting of the mother and child clear lights.

Remaining in the Experience

With knowledge of the identified face of innermost awareness, you should merely sustain or set within it continuously. Thus: "**Be founded in the inexpressible state of the quality of innermost awareness.**"

In other systems of Highest Yoga Tantra, this is called the fundamental innate mind of clear light. Here, in the Great Completeness, within the division into "foundation" and "appearance of the foundation," this is the first, foundational innermost awareness. The innermost awareness that is identified during the operation of the six collections of consciousness — eye, ear, nose, tongue, body, and mental consciousnesses — is vibrant innermost awareness. Through identifying vibrant innermost awareness and sustaining it in meditation, you get down to the foundational innermost awareness.

Dealing with Interference

While meditating this way, experiences of bliss, luminosity, and nonconceptuality can dawn in your mind, but these experiences, which actually are on a coarse level and are not of the most subtle level, as if cover over and obstruct innermost awareness, like a husk over a seed. Therefore, it is necessary to get rid of them. As Patrul Rinpoche says, "**Stability, bliss, luminosity, and delight should again and again be destroyed.**" It is crucial to upend these meditative experiences of not-so-deep bliss, coarse luminosity, and nonconceptuality on a gross level of mind in order to expose innermost awareness in its nakedness. Then it will illuminate from within.

How can they be destroyed? On these occasions, when low-level spiritual experiences come forth, one technique to clear out these interrupting factors is from time to time to shout the syllable PAṬ. Use the syllable in a strong, sharp, short way to remove these coverings over innermost awareness. In the syllable PAṬ, the letter PA represents method that gathers the interrupting factors together, and the letter Ṭ represents wisdom that cuts through and eliminates them. The syllable PAṬ suddenly strikes like lightning, smashing to bits the bark of attachment to meditative experiences. "**Make the syllable of method and wisdom suddenly descend.**"

Inside Meditation and Outside Meditation Are Similar

When you are within inexpressible innermost awareness, you have unimpeded penetration. This means that there is no hindrance or obstruction in the sense that when objects appear in meditation, these appearances need not be stopped. Rather, the mind does not become involved and caught up in appearances of objects; instead, it simply stays in just vivid cognizance of innermost awareness. When this perspective is maintained, the state of meditation called "meditative equipoise" and the state of appearance of objects after meditation called "subsequent attainment" are not very different. Thus, "**Meditative equipoise and subsequent attainment do not differ.**"

While sustaining the face of innermost awareness, there is no such thing as a state of being in a session of meditative equipoise and a state of having risen from meditative equipoise and being outside of a session of meditative equipoise. Whether you are in meditation, keeping your mind on a single object of observation, or not, no matter what so-called state you are in, whatever thought dawns, it just dawns from the vibration of innermost awareness. Once each and every one of these conceptions simply comes from the expanse of innermost awareness, all of them are the sport of innermost awareness, and since they are its effervescence, if you are able to view them from within innermost awareness, they are perforce born within innermost awareness, and as to their place of cessation, they cease in innermost awareness. This is called "recognizing conceptions."

Three Types of Release from Conceptions

The styles of being released from conceptions are three-fold. The first is like passing by a person with whom you are already acquainted. The second is like a snake tied in a knot that unties itself, called the self-release of conceptions. The third is like a burglar entering an empty house — there is nothing for the house to lose and nothing for the burglar to wreck; there is just self-release.

The last is most effective. When, as in the first type, you identify, "A conception has been produced," then even if you have identified it, an apprehension of an object identified and an identifier is involved. Instead, while not fluctuating from sustaining the quality of innermost awareness, if conceptions are produced, let them be produced; if conceptions cease, let them cease. Do not put emphasis on them, ignore them. If you look at their own entity, they are no more than the effulgence, the effervescence, of innermost awareness.

Comprehended from this perspective, conceptions do not pass beyond the vibration of innermost awareness; they do not pass beyond its sport. When viewed from the sphere of innermost awareness, it is of no concern whether conceptions are produced or cease — they neither help nor harm. From this perspective, meditation during a formal session and meditation during times of behavior between sessions are not separate.

Due to maintaining the continuum of realization during meditative equipoise, there should not be any difference between your experience during a meditative session and between sessions. You have an even perspective throughout all states, remaining constantly in self-established placement within innermost awareness. **"Continuously dwelling in the undifferentiable state, session and between-session are not divided."**

The Gradual Way

CONTINUOUS IMMERSION in innermost awareness is the situation for those of extremely sharp faculties, whose karmic endowment is such that hearing an introduction to innermost awareness and being released from obstructions are simultaneous, since these persons can identify innermost awareness and remain within it. However, for beginners, it is usually not sufficient merely to identify innermost awareness; they must meditatively extend this experience through the approach of the gradualist. They must enact repeated meditative familiarity.

For this, the mind needs to be made taut; so it is necessary to give up the busyness of excessive activities until they have attained steadiness by meditating in specified sessions, identifying innermost awareness and sustaining the experience within the set period. Thus, Patrul Rinpoche says, **"However, until attaining stability, meditation within having abandoned commotion is to be valued. Practice is done within division into sessions."**

The Danger

In particular, when leaving the session and engaging in other activities — not when reciting prayers and the like but when meeting people and so forth — meditators are in danger that, due to long acquaintance with powerful afflictive emotions of lust, anger, and obscuration, they will come under the influence of these long-established feelings. Hence, it is extremely important to firmly maintain, at all times and in all circumstances, ascertainment of the experience of having identified innermost awareness — again and again taking it to mind without forgetting it — and to act within this ascertainment.

Our various conceptions induce a variety of good and bad pleasures and pains, all of which in fact do not pass beyond the expanse of the naturally arisen, intrinsically aware, pristine wisdom, which we call the truth body. In terms of their place of origin, these wandering thoughts arise from naturally arisen clear light, and finally, when you arrive at high realization, they dissolve into the same expanse of naturally arisen clear light. In between these, when various appearances dawn like dreams, with such internal knowledge, you must recognize all of them as the display of naturally arisen clear light, the truth body. As Patrul Rinpoche says, **"At all times and occasions, maintain the display of just the truth body."**

Coming to a Decision

Once you gain certainty about this, your mind should not wander about, thinking that this or that practice might be better, touching this and touching that, becoming fractured into many directions. As Shantideva says in the *Guide to the Bodhisattva's Way of Life*, the chance for going deeper will be lost.

Since this is the case, investigate well in the beginning, and then once you have come to a decision, maintain this very one continuously. You should not become scattered by thinking that there is some other practice. **"Be firmly decided that there is none other than this."**

The decision being made is that naked pristine wisdom, the naturally abiding truth body, is a buddha that has never experienced mistake. In the same way, Maitreya's *Sublime Continuum of the Great Vehicle* says:

> The faults are adventitious,
> But the qualities are naturally endowed.

Defilements — the various types of defects — are susceptible to being removed by antidotes. They can be eliminated, they are separable from the mind, and for this reason, they are said to be adventitious. However, the qualities of a buddha are a natural endowment, for the foundation from which they dawn — the naturally arisen innermost awareness or fundamental innate mind of clear light—is primordially established within us, suitable to manifest buddha attributes. We have always integrally possessed the cause, so to speak, of buddha qualities.

In sum, you are to maintain the practice of dwelling—by means of fundamental innate mindfulness—within the innermost awareness identified earlier in your own internal experience, without any differentiation between being inside and outside of meditation. The verse concludes: **"Be determined on this alone—the second essential."**

12

The Third Key
Self-Release

Now, THE LAST of the three keys.

III.

At this time, within knowing the basic entity
Of all desires and hatreds, pleasures and pains,
And all adventitious conceptions, no subsequent
  connection is made.
Through identifying the truth body, the mode of
  release,
They become like writing on water.
With uninterrupted self-appearance and self-release,
Whatever dawns is sustenance for naked empty
  awareness.
Whatever fluctuates is the royal sport of the truth
  body,
Self-purifying without a trace. A LA LA.

The way they dawn is like earlier,
But the modes of release are importantly different.
Meditation without this is a mistaken path.
Those having this, without meditation, are within the
   truth body.
Confidence is found upon release — the third
   essential.

The Space of Noninvolvement

No matter what adventitious or temporary conceptions
are generated — illustrated by lust and hatred, pleasure
and pain — recognize all of them as the mere vibrancy
of innermost awareness. The power of those conceptual
consciousnesses will weaken and will not make connection as they did before, the one after the other, getting
stronger and stronger.

If you are able to sustain well the practice of recognizing innermost awareness, success at training this
way will be helpful even at times of generating strong
desire and hatred, or undergoing strong pleasure from
triumph and strong pain from defeat. For, it is crucial,
in the midst of these emotions, to identify innermost
awareness, the very basis of release. When you are able
to stay within the experience of the already identified basic nature — the true foundation and mode of

release — without losing it, by not fluctuating from it, then conceptions that are generated appear right within the context of this basic nature and thus are like writing on water; they immediately disappear, released in the sphere of innermost awareness, making no connections to subsequent involvement. They melt in their own spot as soon as they are produced. Into what are conceptions released? Into innermost awareness. Having identified basic mind — the Great Completeness, the truth body — into which conceptions are released, then when conceptions themselves appear, they continually release themselves, as if they were written on water.

Through the first key, you have identified innermost awareness, and through the second, you learned to maintain its presence in meditation. Now, the emphasis is on the disappearance of conceptual thought into innermost awareness. "At this time, within knowing the basic entity of all desires and hatreds, pleasures and pains, and all adventitious conceptions, no subsequent connection is made. Through identifying the truth body, the mode of release, they become like writing on water."

Whatever types of conceptions occur, by attending to the empty entity at the core of each of them, recognize them as not passing beyond the nature of fundamental awareness. If you can do this, the machinations of conceptuality itself will assist the practice of sustaining ascertainment of their own reality.

When you are able to sustain this type of practice well, no matter what type of conceptions dawn, they become like sustenance, or food, for naked empty awareness. With conceptions appearing and immediately releasing themselves, they serve to feed and expand the practice of raw, naked, empty awareness. As Patrul Rinpoche says, **"With uninterrupted self-appearance and self-release, whatever dawns is sustenance for naked empty awareness."**

If in this way you do not come under the outside influence of conceptuality but are able to recognize and maintain the natural form of innermost awareness, then no matter how much conceptuality changes, it can dawn to you as the mere vibration, the mere effervescence, of innermost awareness, the royal sport of the truth body, like something merely accompanying fundamental mind.

Due to this, not making any subsequent connection, conceptual thought leaves no imprint. Just as when a bird flies in the sky, it leaves no tracks, so when no matter what conceptions are generated, they become trackless, self-cleansing, they cannot make subsequent connections. **"Whatever fluctuates is the royal sport of the truth body, self-purifying without a trace. A LA LA."** A LA LA is an expression of joy and satisfaction.

The Crucial Difference

When you have such profound experience, conceptions indeed dawn as they did previously, but there is a vast difference in how you are released from them. Despite the fact that thoughts occur much as they did before you identified innermost awareness, you get out of their clutches in vastly different ways. Introduced to reality, in the first stage, you recognize conceptual thoughts like meeting someone with whom you have been acquainted. As soon as a conception is generated, you recognize it, thinking, "Oh, a conception has been produced," which keeps you from coming under its influence. Still, since you are thinking, "This is a conception," the first level of self-release is still involved with a little conceptual apprehension.

On the second level of self-release, thoughts dawn but are unable to make subsequent connection to any further involvement and thus they cannot remain, and so disappear. Conceptuality cannot keep itself going and itself dissolves, like a snake in a knot untying itself; it does not stop due to some other, outside antidote.

On the third, final, and best level of self-release, even if conceptuality is generated, since the face of innermost awareness is being sustained in its own form without being lost, conceptuality cannot do any harm. Maintenance of fundamental mind cannot lose out to it. It is like a robber in an empty house. When a robber slips into an empty house, the empty house has nothing to lose, and the robber has nothing to gain. Conceptuality dissipates by itself.

Of the many such different modes of self-release, the third is the most profound. "**The way they dawn is like earlier, but the modes of release are importantly different.**"

Confidence

Without practicing meditation of unfabricated inner-most awareness, meditation fabricated by conceptuality is merely a practice created by a coarse, temporary, adventitious mind. Such a mind is coarse relative to fundamental innate awareness because it is polluted by conceptuality, and so, in this sense, is a mistaken aware-ness. Therefore, it is said that if you do not have medita-tive practice of unfabricated innermost awareness based in your own experience, you will come under the influ-ence of mistake.

However, if you are able to meditate endowed with such quintessential instructions, you will not need to meditate with mentally fabricated exertion and, instead, will come to confident decisiveness in innermost aware-ness itself, the truth body. "**Meditation without this is**

a mistaken path. Those having this, without meditation, are within the truth body."

Based on confidence that dawns from having experienced self-release, you should place trust in this final
essential. **"Confidence is found upon release — the
third essential."**

13

The Uniqueness of the Three Keys

THE POEM CONCLUDES:

This view endowed with three essential points
Is assisted by and assists meditation entwined with
    exalted knowledge and empathy,
As well as the general deeds of the Victor's children.
Even if the victor presences of the three times
    consulted together,
They would have no guidance exceeding this.
The revealer of the treasure of the truth body from
    the dynamism of innermost awareness
Raised this up as treasure from the vastness of
    wisdom.
Extractions of earth and stone differ from this.
It is the final word of Garab Dorje,
Final extract of the exalted mind of the three
    transmissions.
Restrictedly intended for heart children,

It is the profound meaning.
Conversation of the heart, heart conversation.
Do not lose this essential meaning, essence of
    meaning!
Do not neglect the instructions!

Altruism

The meditation is assisted by training in altruistic deeds motivated by love and compassion. As the poem says, "This view endowed with three essential points is assisted by and assists meditation entwined with exalted knowledge and empathy, as well as the general deeds of the Victor's children."

Patrul Rinpoche emphasizes how the general spiritual path of bodhisattvas, which centers around altruistic deeds inspired by love and compassion, enhances practice of the three keys.

The Greatness of the Path

Until you can make use of the fundamental innate mind of clear light in the path, there is no way at all of attaining buddhahood. Thus, the unique substantial cause of a buddha's omniscience is solely the fundamental innate mind of clear light, innermost awareness. Since the texts of the Great Completeness system explain a technique of quickly experiencing basal innermost awareness in the context of the vibration of innermost awareness even while the six consciousnesses are operating, this is a distinctive feature of the Great Completeness system. From this viewpoint, Patrul Rinpoche says, **"Even if the victor presences of the three times consulted together, they would have no guidance exceeding this."** He thereby indicates the greatness of this path.

Patrul Rinpoche himself is the revealer of this text from the vibration of innermost awareness. Unlike a treasure dug up from the earth, he gathered it as a treasure from the sphere of wisdom, a diamond of naturally arisen innermost awareness. With regard to Old Translation School texts, there are three lineages:

- The distant lineage of the sacred word — the translated texts from India.
- The close lineage of the treasure texts — the texts that the great master Padmasambhava understood would be needed at future times by specific trainees in Tibet, which he then hid, to be revealed by persons endowed with certain karma even a hundred or a thousand years later. When the situation ripens, through the blessings of Padmasambhava himself, and through the force of those persons' merit, karma, and prayer-wishes to reveal such treasure, the treasure text is revealed. Since even after many generations

have passed, direct blessings from Padmasambhava remain, this is called the close lineage.

- The profound lineage of pure visionary experience. Within visionary experience, there are (1) texts that dawn in spiritual experience, (2) texts that dawn to the mental consciousness, and (3) texts that actually dawn to sense consciousnesses.

With his wisdom of innermost awareness, Patrul Rinpoche obtained this text as a revealed treasure from the all-good sphere of the wisdom of innermost awareness. Therefore he says, "**The revealer of the treasure of the truth body from the dynamism of innermost awareness raised this up as treasure from the vastness of wisdom. Extractions of earth and stone differ from this.**"

Such experience dawns suddenly within your own thought as a treasure from the expanse of special realization. It is really amazing, and still occurs nowadays. If someone had to write about these topics by working with conceptual thought, it would be very difficult to compose. However, if you have arrived at naked, all-good, innermost awareness and familiarized with it over many lifetimes, such meditative innermost awareness becomes capacitated such that you can remember experiences from a hundred, a thousand, ten thousand, a hundred thousand lifetimes as if they occurred yesterday, and you can remember teachings that you formerly received that were retained in the expanse of innermost awareness. There is an Old Translation School lama nowadays who has such amazing memories from activating access to the dynamism of innermost awareness — he can recall events from the period of Padmasambhava's presence in Tibet in the eighth century, as well as his own unusual births — fantastic indeed!

Patrul Rinpoche identifies his poem as the final word of the principal Indian guru of the Old Translation School lineage, Garab Dorje: "**It is the final word of Garab Dorje, final extract of the exalted mind of the three transmissions.**" This teaching contains the three transmissions of the Victor Longchen Rabjam, the Omniscient Khyentse Oser Jigme Lingpa, and Jigme Gyalwe Nyugu mentioned at the beginning of the poem. There he made homage to these three great lamas of the Old Translation School tradition, using their names to refer to the view, meditation, and behavior. Since it provides an excellent summary of his text, I have left discussion of it for here:

Homage to the lamas.
The view is the multitudinous great expanse
    (Longchen Rabjam).
The meditation is light rays of knowledge and
    empathy (Khyentse Oser).

The behavior is the shoot of a Victor (Gyalwe
   Nyugu).
For one who practices in this way,
There is no hesitation about buddhahood in one life.
Though not such, amazing blissful awareness!
   A LA LA!

The Triad of View, Meditation, and Behavior

As just mentioned, at the very beginning of the text, the author makes homage to lamas because for this type of practice, called "tantra" and also "mantra," lamas (gurus) are particularly important in general, and especially so in the Great Completeness for someone seeking to practice introduction to naturally arisen innermost awareness. For such a person, faithful respect for lamas is crucial. This being the case, our author, Patrul Jigme Chokyi Wangpo, begins with "**Homage to the lamas**," who are composites of all the sources of refuge from the problems of the round of suffering and finitude.

Because lamas are so important, he speaks of the three topics of view, meditation, and behavior using the names of two of his indirect lamas, Longchen Rabjam ("Multitudinous Great Expanse") and Khyentse Oser ("Light Rays of Knowledge and Empathy," whose other name is Jigme Lingpa), and the name of his own actual immediate lama, Gyalwe Nyugu ("Shoot of a Victor," whose longer name is Jigme Gyalwe Nyugu, a student of Jigme Lingpa). In this way, the author presents the view, meditation, and behavior in connection with the meaning of the names of his indirect and direct lamas. Let me explain these one by one.

THE VIEW, THE MULTITUDINOUS GREAT EXPANSE

The view of reality is the buddha nature beyond the proliferations of dualistic conceptuality. Both the Old Translation School and the New Translation Schools of Tibetan Buddhism speak of the view as the pristine wisdom of clear light, the matrix-of-One-Gone-to-Bliss. The pristine wisdom of clear light itself is not independent and inherently existent but is devoid of conceptual proliferations — an entity pure from the beginning with a spontaneous nature. This pure spontaneous matrix is the basis of appearance of cyclic existence and nirvana, and thus the view itself is the great expanse from which all the multiplications of phenomena dawn and into which all are withdrawn. Thus Patrul Rinpoche says, "**The view is the multitudinous great expanse (Longchen Rabjam).**" In this way, he speaks of the view as "the multitudinous great expanse," which is the meaning of the name of his indirect source-lama, Longchen Rabjam.

The view to be meditated on is the naturally pure buddha nature called the "matrix-of-One-Gone-to-

Bliss," pervading the great vastness, or great expanse, the sphere of reality. The knowledge that all appearances of cyclic existence and nirvana are complete in this equal reality is the view itself—hence the multitudinous, infinite, great expanse, the vastness.

The view of the Great Completeness is said to be beyond mind, but with respect to how it is expressed in words, here "view" mainly refers not to what is viewed but to the viewing consciousness. Thus, it refers to "the viewing subject" not "the view as the object viewed." Still, we must remember that such terms may not be relevant, since the view here is beyond mind, and "subject and object" are bound within the sphere of mind.

All phenomena are contained within the great sphere of innermost awareness, the basis from which all phenomena dawn—the foundation of appearance. From between foundation and appearance, innermost awareness is the foundation, and its vibration is appearance. This, called "All-good innermost awareness," itself is the view, the multitudinous great expanse.

MEDITATION, LIGHT RAYS OF KNOWLEDGE AND EMPATHY

Having engendered this view, one spontaneously generates compassion for sentient beings who, due to ignorance, do not understand this perspective. Thus Patrul Rinpoche says, "**The meditation is light rays**

of knowledge and empathy (Khyentse Oser)." "Light rays of knowledge and empathy" is the very meaning of Khyentse Oser's name. Within the distinction between innermost awareness and the vibration of innermost awareness, the vibration of innermost awareness includes eight types of spontaneous appearance. One of these is all-pervasive compassion—light rays of knowledge and empathy, and from meditation on it, spontaneous factors of leapover, or spontaneous progress, emerge, whereas the multitudinous great expanse is the practice of breakthrough, essential purity.

Upon being introduced to the natural face of innermost awareness in its nakedness, if one is able to dwell in the expanse of innermost awareness by way of fundamental mindfulness, which is a natural innate mindfulness, these spontaneous factors emerge of themselves in meditation. "Nakedness" here means that the obstructive pollution by conceptuality has been removed—conceptuality being like clothing that has been taken off, leaving the naked body, bare awareness.

When experience of innermost awareness emerges, fundamental mindfulness comes along with it, fulfilling the practice of meditation, at which point the practitioner can conclusively decide that what is wanted, liberation, does not pass beyond the expanse of innermost awareness, and what is to be discarded, cyclic existence, does not pass beyond the vibration of innermost awareness. Thereby, both of these—good and bad, nirvana and cyclic existence, hopes and fears—all of these are conclusively seen as the sport, the vibration, and the effervescence of innermost awareness.

BEHAVIOR, THE SHOOT OF A VICTOR

As long as one remains without fluctuating from experience of this unhindered expanse of innermost awareness, no matter what behavior one enacts, it has a single character, like the taste of a single flavor. In this vein, Patrul Rinpoche says, "**The behavior is the shoot of a Victor (Gyalwe Nyugu).**" "Shoot of a Victor" is the very meaning of Gyalwe Nyugu's name. Due to having a compassionate motivation and penetrating wisdom, you engage in altruistic behavior to help others; these altruistically motivated deeds infused with knowledge of reality are the shoot that turns into a buddha.

You need to bring forth the practice of innermost awareness in its own naked state and meditate within that. When you gain such an experiential view, it is not necessary to search for meditation or behavior outside of its scope. When you maintain practice from within the sphere of this view, it is said that

- *The view is left as an unmovable mountain.*
- *Meditation is left as an ocean.* No matter how many waves there are on the surface, the depths remain

stable. When you have been introduced to, and have identified, innermost awareness in experience, then like sun and sunlight, fundamental mindfulness is engendered within it. At this time, you do not need mindfulness achieved from exertion or activity; mindfulness is innate.

- *Behavior is left as appearance.* When you have identified innermost awareness and have experienced this view, then from this perspective, whatever conceptions or objects appear, you do not follow after and get caught up in them but remain vividly within the context of innermost awareness such that it is not necessary to make distinctions between the types of behaviors that are to be adopted and those that are to be discarded, for you are beyond achieving and stopping, hoping and fearing.

If you as a practitioner are able to effectively practice this type of view, meditation, and behavior in the proper way, you have an opportunity to attain buddhahood in this lifetime; it will not be difficult. **"For one who practices in this way, there is no hesitation about buddhahood in one life."**

However, even if you do not achieve buddhahood in this lifetime, through the practice of altruistic motivation and penetrating wisdom, you can be firmly set in high realization such that you will not come under the influence of bad circumstances that might arise during the course of this lifetime. You will not be overwhelmed by strings of hopes and fears but will be able to use bad circumstances in the path, and from lifetime to lifetime, you will proceed from happiness to happiness, able to advance higher and higher. **"Though not such, amazing blissful awareness! A LA LA!"** Even if you do not achieve buddhahood in this lifetime, you will be amazingly happy: "Oh, how wonderful."

The Final Lines of the Poem

At the end of the poem, Patrul Rinpoche gives advice about the importance of this practice, **"Restrictedly intended for heart children, it is the profound meaning. Conversation of the heart, heart conversation. Do not lose this essential meaning, essence of meaning! Do not neglect the instructions!"**

As Dodrubchen says, "Whether realization is produced depends upon your effort." We always have to keep up effort. There is no way you can hope to attain the great easily or quickly.

PART FOUR

The Old and New Translation Schools Compared

14

Basic Structures in the Old Translation School of the Great Completeness

Now LET US discuss two interlocking topics of the Great Completeness, beginning with the two truths, the ultimate truth and conventional truths, and then the triad of basis, paths, and fruits of the paths.

The Two Truths

The clear light nature, basic and luminous, is the final root of all minds — forever indestructible, immutable like a diamond. In Buddhism, this aspect of the mind is considered permanent in the sense that its continuum is uninterrupted — it has always existed and will go on forever and is therefore not something newly started by causes and conditions.

Pure from the start and endowed with a spontaneous

nature, this diamond mind is the basis of all spiritual development. Even while generating a great many good and bad conceptions, such as desire, hatred, and bewilderment, the diamond mind itself is free from the corruptions of these defilements, like sky that exists throughout clouds.

Water may be extremely dirty, yet its nature remains clear. Similarly, no matter what afflictive emotions are generated as the artifice of this diamond mind, and no matter how powerful they are, innermost awareness itself remains unaffected by defilement; it is good without beginning or end.

Wonderful spiritual qualities, such as unbounded love and compassion, are all present in basic form in this diamond mind; their manifestation is prevented only by certain temporary conditions. In a sense, we are enlightened from the very beginning, endowed with a completely good basic mind.

In the Old Translation School tradition of Tibetan Buddhism, the diamond mind is posited as the ultimate truth. This ultimate truth is not posited from the viewpoint of being an object found by a consciousness realizing emptiness, as in the Middle Way School; rather, it is innermost awareness, the clear light having no beginning and no end, the basis of all the phenomena of cyclic existence and of nirvana. Being beyond all adventitious phenomena, it is called the ultimate truth. The sport, manifestations, effervescence, or coarse forms of it are conventional truths.

Even in the New Translation Schools, the fundamental mind also serves as the basis of all the phenomena of cyclic existence and nirvana and is posited as the ultimate truth, the real nature of phenomena. It is also sometimes called the "clear light" and "uncompounded." In the Old Translation School, it is called the "diamond mind"; this is not the mind that is contrasted with innermost awareness in the division into innermost awareness (*rig pa*) and mind (*sems*), but innermost awareness itself, the profound factor of mere luminosity and knowing, the final root of all minds — forever indestructible, immutable, and of an unbreakable continuum like a diamond.

Just as the New Translation Schools speak of a beginningless and endless fundamental innate mind of clear light, the Old Translation School speaks of a diamond mind that has no beginning or end and proceeds without interruption through the fruitional stage of buddhahood. It is considered "permanent" in the sense of abiding forever. It is permanent in that its continuum is not interrupted — this being analogous to the statement in Maitreya's *Ornament for the Clear Realizations* that a buddha's exalted activities are considered permanent in that they are inexhaustible, meaning that their continuum is never severed. Just as a buddha's exalted activities are designated as being "permanent," the clear light also has existed primordially, beginninglessly, without being newly fabricated, continuously abiding, and thus permanently indwelling. The fundamental innate mind of clear light is also uncompounded in that it is not adventitiously and newly produced by causes and conditions.

In general, the term "uncompounded" is understood in two different ways: one is that the clear light is not *at all* put together from causes and conditions, whereas the other is that the clear light is not *newly* fabricated from causes and conditions but has existed primordially, and hence has a continuum that is permanent. Such terms need to be understood in context. For instance, certain wise scholars have said that whatever exists is necessarily "compounded." It may look as if these scholars are denying that permanent phenomena exist since they are not compounded, or made, from causes and conditions, but they are actually saying that all phenomena whatsoever, including the permanent, are established in dependence upon being set up by thought; this is the perspective from which they say that all phenomena are compounded.

Also, it is said that naturally arisen innermost awareness is beyond consciousness, beyond mind. We need to understand that since production, cessation, the compounded, the uncompounded, and so forth, are all within the fence of mental concepts, naturally arisen innermost awareness has a nature *beyond* mind and hence outside the scope of what is posited by terminology and conceptuality. This is why innermost awareness is said to be beyond thought and expression.

Basis, Paths, and Fruits

Let me try to give you an encapsulation of the basis, paths, and fruits according to the Great Completeness. It is complicated, so please bear with me.

THE BASIS: ENTITY PURE FROM THE START AND SPONTANEOUS NATURE

In the Great Completeness, the fundamental structure is threefold — entity pure from the start, spontaneous nature, and compassion:

> The *entity* of innermost awareness is essentially pure, naturally devoid of problems from the start, or in the vocabulary of the Middle Way School, naturally devoid of inherent existence from the very start. Within the sphere of this *nature* of mere luminosity and knowing, all pure and impure phenomena appear as the sport, or manifestation, of its spontaneous nature. All such appearing and

occurring phenomena are characterized by this nature of spontaneity. The unimpeded effulgence of innermost awareness is even called *compassion* because its effect is compassionate activities, risen out of the essentially pure entity and spontaneous nature of the diamond mind.

The first two of these — entity pure from the start and spontaneous nature — are the basis, or foundation, and are central. If we compare this type of vocabulary from the Old Translation School to that of the New Translation Schools, we could say that the vocabulary of "essential purity" refers to the class of emptiness, and spontaneity refers to the class of appearance. Thus, in the Old Translation School, the basis is "essential purity and spontaneity," whereas in other schools the basis is "emptiness and appearance."

Although an association of essential purity with emptiness and an association of spontaneity with appearance can be made, it should be understood that the vocabulary of "essential purity and spontaneity" is used in the context of identifying naturally arisen innermost awareness as the ultimate truth, where "ultimate truth" has a particular meaning in the Old Translation School. Specifically, in the special Old Translation School presentation, ultimate truth is empty of adventitious phenomena, and thus here ultimate truth is an "other-emptiness." This means that ultimate truth, essential purity, is the fundamental innate mind of clear light, which is primordial and fundamental, whereas conventional truths are all other phenomena, which are adventitious in relation to that; ultimate truth is empty of them and thus is an "other-emptiness."

In this way, ultimate truth is itself a union of the emptiness of inherent existence and innermost awareness. Thus, although there are instances when the term "essential purity" is used to refer to innermost awareness, in general, it refers to the emptiness of inherent existence as set forth in Buddha's teaching in what is called the middle wheel of doctrine.

The term "spontaneity" can be identified as referring to the final aim of the thought of the third and final wheel of doctrine, despite not being fully set forth there and despite being fully set forth only in Highest Yoga Tantra. Spontaneous appearance is the final meaning envisioned by the teaching of the buddha nature in the last turning of the wheel of doctrine, this being spontaneous clear light. In this way, these two — "entity pure from the start" and "spontaneity"— are the status of the basis, the foundation.

Without the impact of purity from the very start, defilements could not be adjusted and eventually removed, but even with purity from the start, without the meaning of spontaneity, there would be no way to develop into a buddha. Thus, the basis of the spiritual path comprises essential purity and spontaneity.

THE PATH: BREAKTHROUGH
AND LEAPOVER

The spiritual path is practiced on this basis, the foundation of essential purity and spontaneity. In the context of essential purity, the path of breakthrough is practiced, and in the context of spontaneity, or spontaneous appearance, the path of leapover is practiced.

When a division into the foundation and the appearance of the foundation is made, "purity from the start" and "spontaneity" are the primordially existent innermost awareness that is the basis of all of cyclic existence and nirvana and comprise the situation of the foundation. Then, on the occasion of the path, practices called "breakthrough" are used to meditate on the meaning of purity from the start, and practices called "leapover" are used to enhance increasing levels of unadjusted, nonartificial appearance in the context of spontaneity.

THE FRUITS OF THE PATHS: INWARD
LUMINOSITY AND OUTWARD LUMINOSITY

When, in dependence upon the paths of breakthrough and leapover, their fruits are actualized, the truth body, which is an internal manifestation of purity from the start, and the complete enjoyment body, which is an external manifestation of spontaneity, are actualized. Just as in the basis, there are essential purity and the nature of spontaneity, and at the time of the path there are breakthrough and leapover, so when through the paths of breakthrough and leapover the fruit of practice manifests, there are the essentially pure, inwardly luminous truth body and the spontaneous, outwardly luminous complete enjoyment body.

Purity from the start dawns internally as the truth body, which is experienced in direct perception only among buddhas and does not itself directly appear to trainees, due to which it is called the fulfillment of your own welfare. It manifests only internally to beings endowed with it in their own continuum and is not externally enjoyed by trainees; hence, it is called "purity from the start manifesting internally as the truth body of a buddha." Indeed, the subdivision of the truth body called the "pristine wisdom truth body" entirely revolves around innermost awareness.

Spontaneity externally manifests as the complete enjoyment body of a buddha. For, in reliance upon spontaneous appearances, externally oriented appearances dawn as forms that actually bring about others' welfare; these sometimes are even said to be appearances included in the continuums of the trainees themselves. Based upon spontaneity and in dependence upon the path of leapover, the sport of various pure and impure appearances of emanations dawns in accordance with the interests and dispositions of trainees, these being, respectively, the complete enjoyment body and emanation bodies that manifest externally.

A Special Meaning of "Meditation"

In the Old Translation School, "meditation" on the profound mind means that the mind itself is identifying the profound nature of the mind and sustaining it in meditation but not in the style of meditating *on* an object. When this profound mind identifies itself, just it is manifest. Since, prior to contacting and identifying the entity of this profound mind, you have already ascertained the emptiness of inherent existence of the mind through the practice of breakthrough, watching from what the mind arises, where it abides, and into what it goes, a mind understood as qualified by an emptiness of inherent existence appears.

Even though this can be termed cultivating something more than focusing on a mere absence of inherent existence, this is not like the composite of appearance and emptiness — an elimination of inherent existence that is also an appearance of an object, called "illusory-like appearance" — that is meditated on with a coarser level of consciousness. Rather, the meditation itself proceeds with a subtler mind. As familiarity with innermost awareness grows stronger, the complex of conceptions gradually decreases, consciousness becomes more and more subtle, and the clear light fully manifests.

Even in the New Translation Schools, when the clear light manifests, the emptiness of inherent existence appears. According to the explanation by the New School scholar and adept Norsang Gyatsho, when the clear light appears even to an ordinary person at death, emptiness appears but is not ascertained. For, when any being, even a bug, dies, there is a vanishing of coarse dualistic appearance; it is not that the appearance of inherent existence or conventional appearances vanish but that coarser conventional appearances disappear.

At the time of the clear light of death, emptiness appears but the person, unless he or she is a highly developed yogi, cannot ascertain it because it is not appearing due to the elimination of inherent existence. However, when the mind identifies itself and this is done by a person who has ascertained emptiness, dualistic appearance vanishes, so there is no doubt that this mind is one undifferentiable entity with emptiness; thereby, a vanishing of dualistic appearance into emptiness is fully realized.

GRADUAL DIMINISHMENT OF CONCEPTUALITY

In the Great Completeness, as a yogi grows more and more accustomed to meditating on the composite of emptiness and appearance with a subtle mind — the appearance yet emptiness of this basic mind, the mind being understood as endowed with the emptiness of inherent existence — the appearance of conceptual proliferations gradually diminishes in the sphere of innermost awareness, allowing the very subtle clear light to manifest. For this reason, it is apparent that all the factors involved in cultivating the view of emptiness as presented in the New Translation Schools are contained in Great Completeness meditation.

IDENTIFYING THE CLEAR LIGHT IN THE MIDST OF ANY CONSCIOUSNESS

In the New Translation Schools, actualization of the fundamental innate mind of clear light simultaneous with manifestation of the six operative consciousnesses — the eye, ear, nose, tongue, body, and mental consciousnesses — is said to be impossible. According to the New Translation Schools, it is necessary first to dissolve all coarser consciousnesses, to render them as though incapacitated; only then will the fundamental mind nakedly appear. According to the New Translation Schools, it is impossible for coarse and subtle consciousnesses to occur simultaneously.

In the Old Translation School of the Great Completeness, on the other hand, it is possible to be introduced to the clear light without the cessation of the six operative consciousnesses. Even when an afflictive emotion is generated in an encounter with an object upon which we falsely superimpose a goodness or badness beyond its actual nature, the afflictive emotion itself has the nature of being an entity of mere luminosity and knowing. Since the mind of clear light has the general character of mind as an entity of mere luminosity and knowing, the general factor of the clear light can be identified even in the midst of any coarse afflictive consciousness such as desire or hatred.

As Dodrubchen says, mere luminosity and knowing pervades all consciousnesses and can even be identified during the generation of a strong afflictive emotion without having to cease the six operative consciousnesses. Thus, the difference between the Old Translation School and the New Translation Schools is that when beginning the practice of identifying innermost awareness in the Great Completeness, such stoppage of the six operative consciousnesses is not necessary. Rather, leaving the coarser consciousnesses as they are, the yogi identifies the clear light.

When this identification has been accomplished, it is not necessary purposely to eliminate conceptions of goodness and badness. Instead, no matter what type of conception may arise, it has no power of deception over the practitioner, who is able to remain one-pointedly focused on the feature of mere luminosity and knowing.

Thereby, the conditions for generating the improper mental activity of making false superimpositions upon phenomena diminish in strength, and conceptuality cannot really get started, gradually lessening in strength. In this way, the doctrine of the Great Completeness comes to have a unique mode of presenting the view, meditation, and behavior for someone who has been introduced to innermost awareness and has identified it well.

· 15 ·

Advice

WHEN WE STRIVE for inner development, great achievement is very difficult and almost impossible within a short period; hence, when beginning to practice, we should not expect too much. With a mental attitude of patience and strong determination, as time passes, year by year, inner progress will develop. As a Tibetan lama said, "Suddenly looking at it, it may seem as if it is impossible for someone like oneself to be able to do these things. However, compounded phenomena do not remain as they are; they change with conditions." If we do not become discouraged and keep making exertion, something that we think could not be generated in a hundred years is one day accomplished.

Willpower and determination are essential. Also, while we practice inner development, daily conduct according to moral principles is crucial for the benefit of both ourselves and society.

Some people may feel that this sort of practice is

impractical, or unrealistic. However, even wild animals like tigers and lions can, with patience, be tamed. In that case, we human beings, with such a good brain, such good potential, can tame anything. If we test these practices with patience, we can feel and come to know through our own experience that the mind can be tamed. If someone who easily gets angry tries to control his or her anger, in time it can be controlled. The same is true for a very selfish person; first that person must realize the faults with a selfish motivation and the benefit in being less selfish, and having realized this, he or she trains in it, trying to control the counterproductive side and develop the good side. Implemented in daily life, this sort of practice gradually can be very effective, very valuable.

You can discover whether your mind is tame or not from looking at your behavior. You are your own witness. There are two kinds of witness — others and yourself — but regarding inner development, your own witness is more important.

If those who claim to be practicing doctrines of kindness and so forth lead a good and reasonable life, it is a demonstration, an example, for others to help them realize the value of such practices. People who pretend to practice a system but whose conduct and way of life are not good and reasonable not only accumulate nonvirtue themselves but also harm such teaching in general. Therefore, it is important to be conscientious. This is my appeal.

By being born a human, we have taken on a physical support system through which we can easily achieve both our temporary and our larger aims. Now that we have attained this auspicious life form so unique among the myriad forms born into this world, it is important that we do not waste it. If in this situation, we practice merely to attain a good life in future rebirths for ourselves, we would not be using our potential fully. Or, if we merely aim to liberate ourselves from the tangles of suffering, this would also fall short of our inherent potential. With our humanity, we should do whatever we can to attain perfect, complete spiritual development so that we can be of the greatest benefit to others. At least we should try to be a little kinder.

APPENDIX

Three Keys Penetrating the Core

DZA PATRUL JIGME CHOKYI WANGPO

The full title of Patrul Rinpoche's poem is
The Uniqueness of the Wise Glorious Monarch:
Three Keys Penetrating the Core.

Homage to the lamas.

The view is the multitudinous great expanse (Longchen
   Rabjam).

The meditation is light rays of knowledge and empathy
   (Khyentse Oser).

The behavior is the shoot of a Victor (Gyalwe Nyugu).

For one who practices in this way,

There is no hesitation about buddhahood in one life.

Though not such, amazing blissful awareness! A LA LA!

The view, the multitudinous expanse,

Is cast in practical essentials of three keys.

I.

First set your own mind in a relaxed state,
Not emitting, not withdrawing, without conceptuality.
In this relaxed state of total absorption,
Suddenly shout PAṬ, striking your awareness,
Strong, intense, short. E MA HO!
Not any thing, astounding.
Astounding, unimpeded penetration.
Unimpeded penetration, inexpressible.
Identify innermost awareness of the truth body.
Its entity is identified within yourself — the first
    essential.

II.

Then, whether spreading out or abiding within,
Whether angry or desirous, happy or sad,
At all times and occasions,
Recognize the identified pristine wisdom truth body.
For those with prior acquaintance, the mother and
    child clear lights meet.
Be founded in the inexpressible state of the quality of
    innermost awareness.
Stability, bliss, luminosity, and delight should again and
    again be destroyed.
Make the syllable of method and wisdom suddenly
    descend.

Meditative equipoise and subsequent attainment do
    not differ.
Continuously dwelling in the undifferentiable state,
Session and between-session are not divided.
However, until attaining stability,
Meditation within having abandoned commotion is to
    be valued.
Practice is done within division into sessions.
At all times and occasions,
Maintain the display of just the truth body.
Be firmly decided that there is none other than this.
Be determined on this alone — the second essential.

III.

At this time, within knowing the basic entity
Of all desires and hatreds, pleasures and pains,
And all adventitious conceptions, no subsequent
    connection is made.
Through identifying the truth body, the mode of
    release,
They become like writing on water.
With uninterrupted self-appearance and self-release
Whatever dawns is sustenance for naked empty
    awareness.
Whatever fluctuates is the royal sport of the truth body,
Self-purifying without a trace. A LA LA.
The way they dawn is like earlier,

But the modes of release are importantly different.
Meditation without this is a mistaken path.
Those having this, without meditation, are within the
    truth body.
Confidence is found upon release — the third essential.

This view endowed with three essential points
Is assisted by and assists meditation entwined with
    exalted knowledge and empathy,
As well as the general deeds of the Victor's children.
Even if the victor presences of the three times consulted
    together,
They would have no guidance exceeding this.
The revealer of the treasure of the truth body from the
    dynamism of innermost awareness
Raised this up as treasure from the vastness of wisdom.
Extractions of earth and stone differ from this.
It is the final word of Garab Dorje,
Final extract of the exalted mind of the three
    transmissions.
Restrictedly intended for heart children,
It is the profound meaning.
Conversation of the heart, heart conversation.
Do not lose this essential meaning, essence of meaning!
Do not neglect the instructions!

SELECTED READINGS

H. H. the Dalai Lama. *Becoming Enlightened*. Translated and edited by Jeffrey Hopkins. New York: Atria Books, 2009.

———. *Dzogchen: Heart Essence of the Great Perfection*. Translated by Geshe Thupten Jinpa and Richard Barron (Chökyi Nyima) and edited by Patrick Gaffney. Ithaca, N.Y.: Snow Lion Publications, 2004.

———. *How to Be Compassionate: A Handbook for Creating Inner Peace and a Happier World*. Translated and edited by Jeffrey Hopkins. New York: Atria Books, 2011.

———. *How to Expand Love: Widening the Circle of Loving Relationships*. Translated and edited by Jeffrey Hopkins. New York: Atria Books, 2005.

———. *How to Practice: The Way to a Meaningful Life*. Translated and edited by Jeffrey Hopkins. New York: Atria Books, 2002.

———. *How to See Yourself as You Really Are*. Translated and edited by Jeffrey Hopkins. New York: Atria Books, 2006.

———. *Kindness, Clarity, and Insight*. Translated and edited by Jeffrey Hopkins; coedited by Elizabeth Napper. Ithaca, N.Y.: Snow Lion Publications, 1984. Revised edition, 2006.

———. *The Meaning of Life: Buddhist Perspectives on Cause and Effect*. Translated and edited by Jeffrey Hopkins. Boston: Wisdom Publications, 2000.

———. *Mind of Clear Light: Advice on Living Well and Dying Consciously*. Translated and edited by Jeffrey Hopkins. New York: Atria Books, 2003. Previously published in hardcover as *Advice on Dying*.

Hopkins, Jeffrey. *Mi-pam-gya-tsho's Primordial Enlightenment: The Nyingma View of Luminosity and Emptiness, Analysis of Fundamental Mind*. With oral commentary by Khetsun Sangpo. Dyke, Va.: UMA Institute for Tibetan Studies, 2015. uma-tibet.org.

———. *Nagarjuna's Precious Garland: Buddhist Advice for Living and Liberation*. Ithaca, N.Y.: Snow Lion Publications, 1998.

———. *A Truthful Heart: Buddhist Practices for Connecting with Others*. Ithaca, N.Y.: Snow Lion Publications, 2008.

Khetsun Sangpo Rinpoche. *Tantric Practice in Nyingma*. Translated and edited by Jeffrey Hopkins; coedited by Anne Carolyn Klein. Ithaca, N.Y.: Snow Lion Publications, 1983.

Mi-pam-gya-tso. *Fundamental Mind: The Nyingma View of the Great Completeness*. With practical commentary by Khetsun Sangpo Rinbochay. Translated and edited by Jeffrey Hopkins. Ithaca, N.Y.: Snow Lion Publications, 2006.

Rinchen, Geshe Sonam, and Ruth Sonam. *Yogic Deeds of Bodhisattvas: Gyel-tsap on Āryadeva's Four Hundred*. Ithaca, N.Y.: Snow Lion Publications, 1994.

Tsong-kha-pa. *The Great Treatise on the Stages of the Path to Enlightenment*. 3 vols. Translated and edited by Joshua W. C. Cutler and Guy Newland. Ithaca, N.Y.: Snow Lion Publications, 2000–2004.

Wallace, Vesna A., and B. Alan Wallace. *A Guide to the Bodhisattva Way of Life*. Ithaca, N.Y.: Snow Lion Publications, 1997.

INDEX